CODES & CIPHERS

HUNDREDS OF UNUSUAL AND SECRET WAYS TO SEND MESSAGES

Also by Christina Ashton:

Words Can Tell: A Book About Our Language
(Simon and Schuster, 1988)

CODES & CIPHERS

HUNDREDS OF UNUSUAL AND SECRET WAYS TO SEND MESSAGES

CHRISTINA ASHTON

BETTERWAY BOOKS
Cincinnati, Ohio

Typography by Blackhawk Typesetting

Illustrations by Studio 500

97 96 95 94 93   5 4 3 2 1

Library of Congress Cataloging-in-Publication Data

Ashton, Christina.
    Codes and ciphers : hundreds of unusual and secret ways to communicate / Christina Ashton. — 1st ed.
        p. cm.
    Includes index.
    Summary: Provides the history behind codes and ciphers as used in spying and explains how readers themselves can make and use their own secret codes.
        ISBN 1-55870-292-X : $7.95
        1. Cryptography—Juvenile literature. 2. Ciphers—Juvenile literature. [1. Cryptography. 2. Ciphers.] I. Title.
Z103.3.A83   1993
652'.8—dc20   92-39008
                                                              CIP
                                                               AC

For Justin Christopher Ellis

.

Contents

1
35421
(Codes)

DEATH NOTICE

One day in 1985, a death notice appeared in *The London Times*. It said:

> VON HESSEN. On August 21 at Penzance, Cornwall. Timothy, Mark, and James. Dearly beloved sons of Margarita, Countess von Hessen and the late Count Richardt. Funeral services to be held in Germany. Donations to the NSPCC.

What a terrible tragedy! All three sons dead at once! What could have happened? And why were donations to go to the NSPCC, the National Society for the Prevention of Cruelty to Children?

Editors of the *Times* were curious at first, and then downright suspicious. They began to investigate. What they discovered was that Timothy, Mark, and James were not dead. As a matter of fact, they had never existed, and there was no such person as Margarita, Countess von Hessen. After further investigation by Scotland Yard, British authorities concluded that this death notice was actually a message in code. No one was certain exactly what the message meant, but it was known that there was a great deal of spying going on between East and West Germany. At that time, East Germany was under Communist leadership. Authorities concluded that the death notice was a warning to East German agents operating in England, telling them to go under cover.

People have been spying on each other for centuries, and messages in code and cipher are as old as reading and writing. Spies are the people most likely to use codes and ciphers for secret communication, but many other people use them, too, and not only for secrecy. Codes are frequently used for convenience, and sometimes, just for fun.

Nations' governments often communicate with each other in diplomatic code, not only to keep their messages secret, but also because coded messages are shorter and more convenient. The armed forces use naval and military codes. Business communication is often written in code for both convenience and secrecy. Secret societies and criminal organizations have been known to devise special codes and ciphers to keep their activities secret from the rest of the world.

Today, in the age of the computer, the average citizen uses codes for many things. Some are secret, some are not. The zip code on an address, for example, is no more than a convenient way to write the state, area of the state, city, and section of the city where a person lives. Average citizens use secret codes every day to access computers in automatic tellers to do their banking. The "computer languages" — the letters, numbers, and symbols used to program computers — are all types of codes. Finally, there are hundreds of people who experiment with codes and ciphers just for the fun of it, because they enjoy mysteries and puzzles.

Although government security regulations make it impossible for the general public to learn much about modern day secret diplomatic and military codes, history and literature provide many fascinating stories in which communication plays an important part. In this book, we will look at some of the secret writing of the past and learn how to make and break some ciphers for ourselves.

"HE HAS A WEIRD VOICE"

The death notice in the London *Times* is an example of open code. It is the use of everyday language to mean something other than what it seems. Since the words have a special meaning known only to the sender and receiver, there is no need to hide the message; it can be "in the open." Throughout history, especially during wartime, open codes have been scratched on bark, carved in stone, written in correspondence, printed in newspapers, and much later, sent by telegraph and broadcast over the radio.

Frequently, in cases where communication is to be top secret, people, places, things, and activities are given code names. Just before World War II, the Germans invented a coding machine which was called *enigma*. The British broke the codes in that machine and called their version of them *Ultra*. *Ultra* is known as one of the best-kept secrets of World War II. The Japanese invented a code and coding machine called *Purple*. The Americans broke that code and called their version *Magic*. The *Black Code* was used by the Americans to communicate information to the United States government about World War II battles between the British and the Germans in North Africa.

Admiral Q was the code name for Franklin D. Roosevelt, the U.S. President during World War II. Winston Churchill, Prime Minister of Great Britain at that time, was known as *Colonel Warden*. Battle plans, or operations, were all given code names. *Operation Sealion* was the code name for a German plan to invade England. The invasion never took place because German Chancellor Adolph Hitler changed his mind. It was the British *Ultra* that uncovered both the plan for *Sealion* and the decision to scrap it. Plans for the Normandy invasion, the battle that was the beginning of the end of World War II in Europe, were called *Operation Overlord*. The American part of that operation was called *Cobra*, and the British involvement was called *Goodwood*. Some other code words used during World War II were:

Dracula	The British capture of Rangoon, Burma from the Japanese
Crossbow	The British defense against German missiles known as V Rockets
Gee	Radar aid to the navigation of bombers
Strangle	Air attacks on railroads in Northern Italy
Tube Alloys	Atom bomb research
Zip	An order from the commander-in-chief to begin an operation

There are many more World War II code words that are common knowledge, but, we suspect, there are just as many more which are still kept secret.

Code words were not only used separately to name things, they were also used to convey whole messages. In England during World War II, many telephone lines were destroyed by bombing raids. The BBC (British Broadcasting Corporation) would broadcast personal messages over the radio to people who did not have telephone service. Mixed in with these messages were coded messages directed to civilians who carried secret information to the fighting forces. A warning to go under cover or the notice of an attack could be broadcast as: "From Emma to John. I cannot go to the theater tonight." It sounded like all the other messages, but could mean the difference between life and death, victory and defeat. One of the messages of some importance to this secret activity was, "He has a weird voice." This phrase was used in longer messages to alert the British forces that the rest of the message had vital information in it.

WHERE IN THE WORLD IS NUTSI?

Open codes are not always as secure as they could be. For one thing, several people have to know what the words mean, and it is all too easy to give away the information accidentally to the wrong person. For another, someone might make a mistake in sending or receiving the message. In wartime, mail sent from battle sites is censored. That means that anything in a letter that might give away secret information is crossed out. To get around this, people write to each other in open code. Sometimes censors are too clever to be fooled. During World War II, a man in Germany sent a letter to his brother in America in which there was the sentence, "Father is dead." The German censor suspected this might be a code phrase. So he changed it to read: "Father is deceased," and sent it on to America. Soon the American reply came back. The censor opened it and read, "Father is *dead* or *deceased*?" Now, in plain language, dead and deceased mean the same thing. In code, obviously, they meant something quite different from each other. When the censor saw the question, he knew secret information was going out of Germany and was able to help uncover the operation.

Sometimes an open code fails, because, through no one's fault, things just go wrong. During World War II, the American War Office censored letters from soldiers and sailors who were stationed in places that had to be kept secret from the enemy. One soldier wanted to get around this regulation. Before he went overseas, he told his parents he would address letters to them with a different middle initial in his father's name on the envelopes. These initials would spell out the name of the place where he was stationed. He was sent to Tunis in North Africa. Over a period of time, he wrote his parents five letters, the first addressed to Mr. John T. Smith, the second to Mr. John U. Smith, and so on, until TUNIS had been spelled out. But the young man forgot how unreliable wartime mail can be. He did not number his letters, and although his parents received all five of them, the letters did not arrive in the order he sent them. The first one they received was addressed to Mr. John N. Smith. Then came letters addressed: Mr. John U. Smith, John T., John S., and John I. Although his parents searched and searched in atlases, nowhere in the world could they find a place called NUTSI.

No one realized it at the time, but NUTSI is an anagram for TUNIS. An anagram is a scrambled word. Making and solving anagrams is a popular word game. If you ever try to solve the word jumbles on a newspaper game page, you are playing anagrams. People like to put messages and slogans into anagrams just for the fun of it. Presbyterians, for example, are happy to point out that PRESBYTERIAN is actually an anagram for BEST IN PRAYER. In 1936, Franklin D. Roosevelt was the democratic candidate for U.S. President. His Republican opponent was Alfred Landon. One Republican wrote an anagram for Roosevelt's name. He scrambled the letters FRANKLIN DELANO ROOSEVELT to read: VOTE FOR LANDON 'ERE ALL SINK. The mysterious message, WHERE CAN I SIGN ODD SCRIPT? is an anagram for WRITING CODES AND CIPHERS.

There is a difference between codes and ciphers. Codes use plain language to mean something other than the obvious, as we saw in the case of the death notice, or they substitute groups of letters or numbers for whole words. Here is an example of a substitution code. It is fictitious, but could be a page from a code book. A code book is a kind of dictionary that explains what the groups of letters and numbers mean.

Plain text	Code No.	Code Word
at	1640	QJLO
battle	1934	BXNA
beach	1876	DLFP
dawn	1066	ZDMA
north	8019	XGLY
on	3524	RMZO
place	2031	HTBN
send	4795	SVJD
south	7767	LXAW
take	5912	BQDY
time	6342	TMSH
to	8405	WMXA

The message BATTLE TO TAKE PLACE AT DAWN ON NORTH BEACH would be: 1934 8405 5912 2031 1640 1066 3524 8019 1876 or: BXNA WMXA BQDY HTBN QJLO ZDMA RMZO XGLY DLFP. The title of Chapter One of this book is a number code for the word "codes."

Ciphers deal with single letters rather than whole words. There are substitution ciphers and transposition ciphers. An anagram, or scrambled word, is a transposition cipher. The young soldier stationed in Tunis thought he was sending a message in code, but he was actually sending a transposition cipher. There will be more about ciphers later in this book.

Any message written in code or cipher is called cryptogram from the Greek word *kryptos*, which means "hidden." To put a message into cipher is to encipher, and to translate a cryptogram is to decipher. If the message is to be in code, it is encoded and decoded. The study and design of codes and ciphers is called cryptography. People who work with codes and ciphers are called cryptographers and cryptanalysts.

Secret communication goes on all the time, but more often in wartime than in peacetime. In wartime, secret messages have had a great impact on history. On the following pages are some real-life examples of how codes had great influence on the outcome of wars. They are stories of human courage and skill, and also of human error.

THE VIOLINS OF AUTUMN

Operation Overlord was the code name for the invasion of Normandy, France in 1944, during World War II. Early in the war, in 1940, the Germans invaded and occupied France. The commander-in-chief of the German forces in France by 1944 was Field Marshall Erwin Rommel. *Operation Overlord* was to be the mightiest attack of combined forces in the history of warfare. Soldiers, sailors, and airmen from the United States, Great Britain, Canada, Australia, and New Zealand were to come together in a combined invasion of France in order to drive the Germans back and defeat them. This combined force, known as the Allies, was commanded by the American general, Dwight D. Eisenhower.

Many French people were resigned to the German occupation of the country, but many were not. Those who were not organized themselves into a group called the Resistance. The Resistance spied on the Germans, received and passed secret information to the Allies, and performed acts of sabotage on the Germans.

The Normandy invasion eventually took place on June 6, 1944, a day known as D-Day. But almost up to the last moment even Eisenhower himself could not be sure exactly when it would take place. The weather was terrible the days immediately before D-Day, more like midwinter than the month of June. The fog was so thick visibility was nearly zero, and the seas were so rough ships could not approach the Normandy coast to land the troops.

Hour after hour, in their headquarters in England, Allied officers waited in shivering suspense for the weather to break. Exact timing was essential, because all air, land, and sea forces had to be coordinated to attack at precisely the same time, and the French Resistance had to be notified when to begin their sabotage attacks on German installations. Never before had there been such great need for secure, swift, unbreakable codes, and quick thinking people ready to spring into action or change plans at a moment's notice.

As we have mentioned, it was the practice of the BBC to broadcast coded messages concerning enemy activity. The BBC also broadcast dummy messages — messages that were meant for the enemy to intercept and decode in order to distract them from the real message. By

1944, cryptanalysts of all warring nations were in a frenzy of intercepting, decoding, and interpreting messages. It was harder and harder to maintain security, because most codes had been broken, and everyone was reading everyone else with relative ease. The most secure way to pass a message at that time was by open code. But even open codes were all too often intercepted and decoded. In the case of the Normandy invasion, the Germans did indeed intercept and decode the two most vital messages connected with the operation, but they misinterpreted them.

As D-Day approached, the BBC was regularly broadcasting weather reports and general instructions to the French Resistance. The open codes were made up of any phrase or sentence that suited a person's fancy. Often they were quotations from literature. The two messages signaling the beginning of the Normandy invasion were lines from a well-known French poet and were broadcast by the BBC in French. They were *"Les sanglots longues des violins de l'automne."* In English this means, "The long sobs of the violins of autumn" and was a code phrase for "Stand by. Invasion imminent." The other line was, in French, *"Blessent mon coeur d'une langeur monotone"* which means, more or less, "My heart is wounded with a monotonous languor." That was code for: "Invasion begun. Start sabotage operations."

Now here is the astonishing part of the story. Rommel was given the translation and thought "imminent," which means "just about to happen," actually meant "in about two weeks time." So, after reading the message, he set it aside and went home to celebrate his wife's birthday. A fatal error. Not knowing how Rommel had interpreted the first message, German radio operators continued to listen for the second one. They intercepted and decoded it and gave it to the man commanding in Rommel's absence. The officer thought the message was a dummy and did not act on it immediately. Another fatal error. The message finally did reach the German forces, but only three hours before the first Allied troops entered Normandy, far too late for Germany to prepare any kind of defense. The French Resistance had performed its sabotage, and the Germans were severely beaten.

Many historians believe that if the Germans had acted upon the information as late as 48 hours before the invasion they might have had a

chance to beat the Allies. As it was, "the violins of autumn" played a funeral hymn for Germany, for by May 1945, she surrendered, and the war was over in Europe.

THE DESERT FOX

Before Field Marshal Erwin Rommel was put in command of the German forces in France, he was commander of the campaign in North Africa. There is no question that Rommel was an excellent officer. He had a record of many victories behind him. He was so clever at battle tactics, particularly in North Africa, that he was known as the Desert Fox. In 1941, the British forces in North Africa outnumbered Rommel's three to one, yet Rommel always seemed one step ahead of them and could avoid surprise attacks, regroup his forces, and attack the British instead. The British began to lose battle after battle. Rommel's foreknowledge of British positions seemed supernatural.

This was all happening before the United States entered World War II. But the Americans were sympathetic to the British side, and helped it in every way they could, short of actually fighting. One thing they did was observe the action in North Africa and transmit information to the British and American embassies and back to the battlefield. The messages were in a code known as the Black Code.

The man in charge of transmitting this sort of information was an American colonel whom we will call Colonel B. It is thought that Colonel B. might have suspected that the Germans were listening in on the messages he sent from his post in Cairo, Egypt, but he was so sure of the security of the Black Code, he was not worried. He should have been, because actually, several months earlier, the Italians had broken into the American Embassy in Rome and stolen the code.

Although Colonel B. did not know it, the Italians were reading everything the Americans were transmitting, and the Black Code was no more secret than the words you are reading right now. Technically, the Italians were allies of the Germans, but they were not very friendly allies. They sent Rommel the information they decoded and one part of the Black Code, but not the whole code. The Germans had to rely on the Italians for all their information, and this took far too long to get the information to Rommel to do him any good. The Germans would have to break the code themselves. And they did, just at the moment that Colonel B. was transmitting information about British positions in the desert. How were they able to do it? Colonel B. made a serious error when he used the code. That error, plus having the part of the code revealed to them by the Italians enabled the Germans to break the code and get the information to Rommel in time to beat the British in so many battles. So the Desert Fox was sly enough on his own, but not so sly as to win his battles without the help of a broken code. Here is what happened:

The Black Code was a number substitution in two parts. If a message began: TO AGWAR BRITISH TO WITHDRAW 270 PLANES FROM COMBAT AREA, the code message would be: 19307 59270 34975 10087 61924 77590 82134 55183. But it was more complicated than that. When the message was transmitted, each number group was changed by the addition of another number group to it. For example, 15000 would be added to each number group and the sums would be the numbers that were actually sent. The second number, in this case 15000, would be changed every day. The numbers were added without carrying. For example, 19307 plus 15000 normally would be 34307. But for the purpose of this code, the sum of those two numbers would be 24307. Here is how the whole process worked:

Message	TO AGWAR BRITISH TO WITHDRAW 270 PLANES FROM COMBAT AREA						
1st part:	19307	59270	34975	10087	61924	77590	82134	55183
2nd part:	15000	15000	15000	15000	15000	15000	15000	15000
Code sent:	24307	64270	49975	25087	76924	82590	97134	60183

Because the Italians sent the Germans only part of the code, the Germans knew that 61924 meant "planes," but did not know that "planes" was actually transmitted as 76924 (61924 + 15000). But then Colonel B. made his error. For some reason he always began his messages the same way, TO AGWAR. AGWAR was an abbreviation of Adjutant General, War Office. Therefore his messages always began with the same code number, 19307. If the second number were 15000, then the message always began 24307. Having the partial code, the Germans were eventually able to deduce that by subtracting

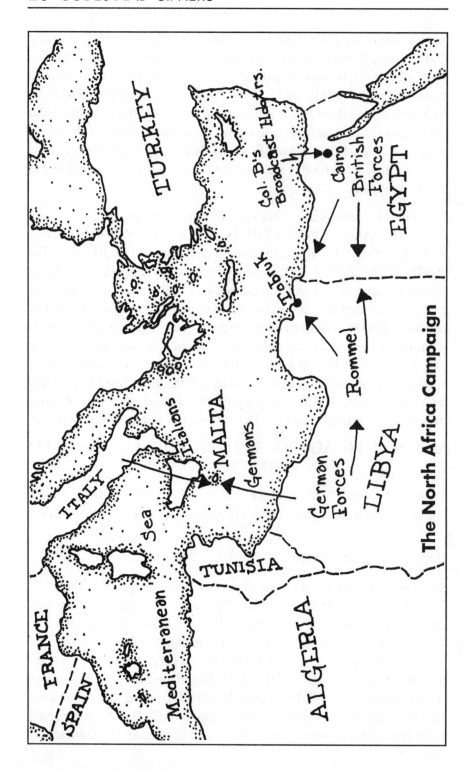

The North Africa Campaign

19307 from 24307 they would get the second code number, no matter what it was. Then all they had to do was subtract the second number from all the other numbers and they would have the basic Black Code. As long as Colonel B. continued to address his messages the same way it did not matter what the second number was. It could be 29873, 41869 — anything. Each time, the Germans could subtract 19307 from it, and then subtract that answer from the other numbers in the message. Within two hours of receiving the message, they could decode it, put it into a German code and transmit it to Rommel. From then on, therefore, Rommel always had plenty of time to outwit the British.

Many of the circumstances surrounding the secret messages transmitted during the North Africa Campaign still remain shrouded in mystery. It is an interesting coincidence that Rommel began to lose to the British about the same time that Colonel B. stopped broadcasting. It is also true that at the same time Colonel B. stopped broadcasting the Americans discovered that the Black Code had been broken, and they stopped using it. Many cryptographers today believe that if Colonel B. had not always addressed his messages in exactly the same way, the Germans never would have been able to break the Black Code. The fact is, as long as it was being used, the Desert Fox was as sly as sly could be, and when it was no longer being used, the Fox was run to ground.

ADMIRAL YAMAMOTO AND JN 25

On Sunday morning, December 7, 1941, the Japanese launched a surprise aerial attack on the American naval base at Pearl Harbor, Hawaii. This brought the United States into World War II, which had already been going on in Asia since 1937, and in Europe since 1939. It took the United States nearly two years to recover from this initial defeat and turn the tide of war against Japan.

The mastermind of the Pearl Harbor attack was Admiral Yamamoto. He was killed in 1943 when his plane was shot down by the Americans. Efficient cryptography enabled the Americans to determine the location of his plane at a particular time.

Sometime around 1942, the Japanese devised an ingenious code that was even more complex than Code Purple, which they had invented some five years before that. A combination of numbers and Japanese characters, it was called JN 25. It was particularly difficult for Americans to decode because there were so few cryptographers who had both security clearance and a knowledge of Japanese. Those code breakers who knew some Japanese kept a record of the characters they had already translated to use as a point of comparison for the characters in other messages. This is what JN 25 looked like:

20463	合 戸, 戸
40811	洽 F
86660	洽
04069	武 米 民 空
12951	
44135	９F
58361	武

In this code, the most significant number is 44135. The characters next to it do not stand for the meanings of words and phrases as the others do, but stand for a code group, a code within a code, called GF. GF stands for groups of letters which are codes for geographical locations. Battles in the war with Japan were fought throughout hundreds of tiny islands in the Pacific Ocean. Because there were so many islands, knowing the code names for exact geographical locations was extremely important. Although the Americans were able to determine that the GF group contained codes for the names of geographical locations, they did not know which letters or letter combinations stood for which location. But they found out, in this way:

The Americans sent dummy messages — messages they knew would be intercepted and decoded by the Japanese. For example, they would send a message saying, "Water is in short supply on Midway Island." They would then monitor the Japanese communication until they picked up a message that was conveying the same information to

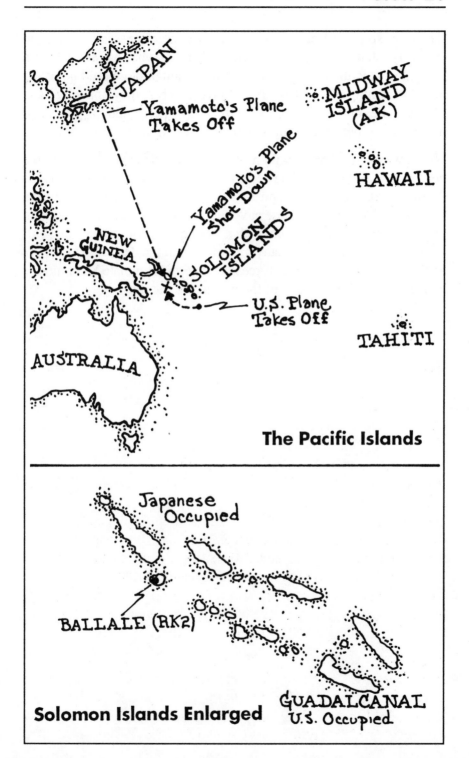

The Pacific Islands

Solomon Islands Enlarged

Japanese ships and planes. When the Japanese message referred to Midway Island as AK, the Americans learned what AK stood for. In a similar way, the Americans knew that Yamamoto would be flying on the morning of April 18, 1943 to RKZ. RKZ, they knew by then, was Ballale, in the Solomon Islands. They intercepted his plane and shot it down before it could reach its destination.

There was no one who could replace the excellence of Yamamoto's leadership. Not only had he been a brilliant naval officer, he had also been a source of great inspiration to his men. With his death, the fighting spirit of the Japanese navy seemed to weaken, and their battle strategy never again matched that of the surprise attack on Pearl Harbor. It is believed by many historians that the decoding of JN 25, which enabled the American forces to locate and eliminate Yamamoto's plane, changed the course of the war in the Pacific.

2

(Ciphers)

A ZILLION WAYS TO SAY THE SAME THING

Ciphers, which deal with separate letters rather than whole words, fall into two groups: substitution ciphers, which are made up of symbols, numbers, or other letters in place of normal letters in the alphabet; and transposition ciphers, which scramble the order of normal letters, as in an anagram.

Enciphering a cryptogram into a transposition cipher is a simple thing to do, but it can take a long, long time, because there are countless ways you can scramble and rearrange letters. A three-letter word like PAL, for instance, can be written six different ways: PAL, ALP, LAP, PLA, APL, AND LPA.

André Langie, a famous French cryptographer, calculated that a group of twenty letters could be arranged 2,432,902,007,246,400,000 ways — let's say a zillion ways, give or take a billion or two. Langie further calculated that if a cryptanalyst spent one second on each combination he would finish his work in 75,000,000,000 (75 billion) years!

Now, if it takes a person so long to design a transposition cipher, how long would it take someone to decipher it? Certainly, it would take too long for the message to be of any use. The trick is to decide on one or two patterns that are known to both sender and receiver. If if is to be a secret message, the pre-arranged letter patterns must be kept secret from everyone else, of course. Suppose you want to send the message:

UNDER COVER. Arrange the letters on two lines, like this:

U		D		R		O		E
	N		E		C		V		R

Then write out the message like this: UDROE NEVCR. The receiver of the message deciphers it in this way: Place the first letter of the top letter group on one line, the first letter of the under group next to it, the second letter of the top group next to that, and so on. In short, the receiver reverses the process. Transposition ciphers can be very complicated, especially if there is a need for secrecy, but they are all based on the idea of some very simple rearrangement.

"OFF WITH YOUR BELT!"

As far as we know, the first transposition cipher was used by the ancient Greeks about 2300 years ago. At that time, Greece was not a unified nation, but a collection of city-states. The neighboring land of Persia, now Iran, was building a great empire then and was constantly making war on Greece, trying to swallow up the city-states, one by one.

Lysander, king of the city-state of Sparta, had reason to believe that Persia was soon to attack his land. Persia had been his ally in the past, but now he was not so sure of her friendship. So he sent spies into Persia to try to find out one way or the other. Later, he sent one of his slaves to meet with the spies and bring back information. Weeks went by, and the slave did not return. Lysander was near panic. Without that information he did not know whether to risk losing Persia's friendship by preparing for war, or risk losing his kingdom by *not* preparing for war.

At last the slave arrived. He was dirty and exhausted from his long secret journey on foot from Persia. His clothes were in rags, held together only by a leather belt around his waist. Before he collapsed in exhaustion at Lysander's feet he drew from his belt that all important letter. But to the slave's astonishment, Lysander threw the letter aside and cried, "Off with your belt!"

On the inner side of the belt was a row of jumbled letters. To anyone else they might have been gibberish, but to Lysander they would reveal a clear message. He fastened one end of the belt to his royal scepter and then very carefully wound the belt around his scepter. At each turn of the belt letters appeared next to each other in sensible order until the whole message was spelled out. It was as Lysander had suspected. Persia *was* planning an invasion of Sparta. Luckily, the faithful slave had returned in time, and Lysander was able to defend Sparta from the Persian invasion.

The scepter and the belt together are known as a *scytale* (rhymes with Italy). You can make a scytale yourself, but you do not need a royal Spartan scepter and slave's belt. You can make one with a pencil and a strip of paper. Or, if you prefer to work with something square, you can use a box or a book to wrap the paper around. The important thing is that the person to whom you are sending the message has the exact same size and shape object as you have used. Otherwise, the message won't read out correctly.

Here is how to make a scytale with a pencil and a strip of paper. Cut a strip of paper 1/4 inch wide and about 12 inches long. Fasten one end of the paper to one end of the pencil with tape. Now wind the paper carefully around the pencil, overlapping each section once. When you have wound the whole strip, fasten the end of it to the pencil with tape.

Now, beginning at the left, write your message horizontally across the length of the pencil, just as if you were writing across a sheet of paper. Suppose your message is MEET ME AT SIX. Write it out across the pencil. Do not leave spaces between words. Turn the pencil once and write a meaningless jumble of letters, each letter exactly under each letter in the message. Like this:

M	E	E	T	M	E	A	T	S	I	X
O	X	P	L	N	Y	T	Z	O	L	Y
J	N	G	E	T	O	P	X	N	P	Z

Write a line of letters at each turn of the pencil until you are back at the original message. Now peel off the tape and unwind the strip of paper. When your friend receives the message, he or she will be able to read it by winding it around a pencil *exactly the size and thickness* of the pencil you used. Figures 1, 2, and 3 show how a scytale is made.

Two thousand years after Lysander, around 1790, Thomas Jefferson devised a simple machine based on the principle of the scytale.

The Scytale

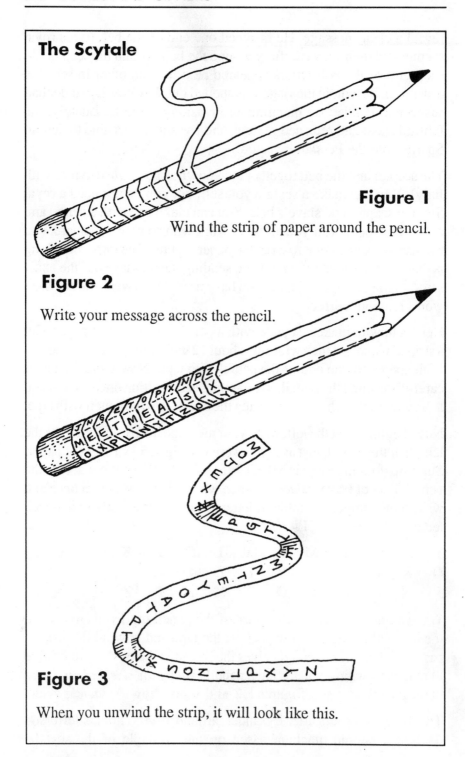

Figure 1

Wind the strip of paper around the pencil.

Figure 2

Write your message across the pencil.

Figure 3

When you unwind the strip, it will look like this.

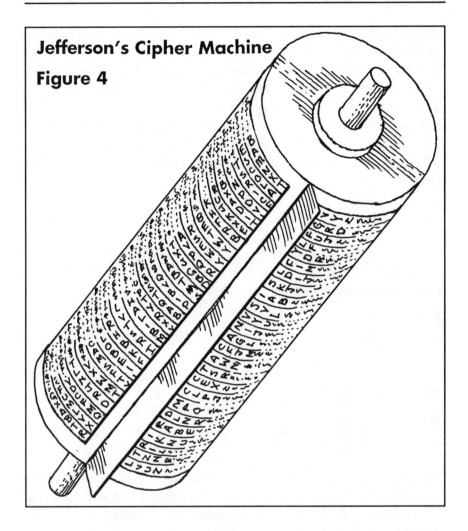

Jefferson's Cipher Machine

Figure 4

Jefferson took a spindle and placed on it 25 wooden discs. On each disc were the 26 letters of the alphabet written in jumbled order. If he wanted to send the message HAVE RECEIVED YOUR LETTER, he would turn the first disc until the letter H appeared. He would then turn the second disc until the A appeared next to the H. Once the message was spelled out all the other lines were in jumbled order. Jefferson then copied down any one of these jumbled lines as his cipher message. The receiver would arrange this jumble on his own spindle and then read all the other lines until he came to the plain language message. Figure 4 shows Jefferson's machine.

Another type of transposition cipher is the square or rectangle, called that because the message is written out in a rectangular pattern. The cipher is based on a key word. Having a key word saves the cryptographer 75 billion years of trying to design and solve scrambled words. This is how it works: Let's say you want to send the message SCRAP THE MISSION, and you have decided on the key word MUSIC. To each letter of the key word assign a number according to where the letter appears in the alphabet. C is closest to A, so C=1, I=2, M=3, S=4, U=5.

3	5	4	2	1
M	U	S	I	C

Your message has 15 letters in it, and your key word has 5. So you are going to begin enciphering by writing out the message in a rectangle made of three rows of 5 letters each:

Key:	3	5	4	2	1
	M	U	S	I	C

Message: SCRAP THE MISSION

Row 1	S	C	R	A	P
Row 2	T	H	E	M	I
Row 3	S	S	I	O	N

Next, take the letters under C, which is number 1, and write them thus: PIN. Next to that, write the letters of group 2, AMO. Continue with groups 3, 4, and 5 until your message looks like this: PINAMOSTSREICHS.

To decipher the message, the receiver must write out the key word, assign the numbers to the letters and turn the message back into columns, beginning with the M column, which is the third group of the cipher (STS), continuing with U, the fifth group, then S, the fourth group, and so on, until the enciphering process is reversed and the message comes clear.

This is known as a "low security" cipher, because it is relatively easy for an experienced cryptanalyst to break it. The best way to make this kind of cipher as secure as possible is to choose a key word that might be hard to guess but easy to memorize. Any word or phrase will do for a key, as long as no letter in it is used more than once. If the number of words in your message and the number of letters in your key do not work out to a square or even a rectangle, fill in the leftover spaces with extra letters that are meaningless, that have nothing to do with the message. Such fill-ins are called nulls. The message SEND MONEY SOON, based on the word HELP, would work out into a square of four letters across and four letters down with three nulls.

Key: 2   1   3   4
         H   E   L   P

Message: SEND MONEY SOON

Row 1	S	E	N	D
Row 2	M	O	N	E
Row 3	Y	S	O	O
Row 4	N	L	X	P

The message would read EOSLSMYNNNOXDEOP, with L, X, and P being nulls.

Try this cipher: Your key word is BUGS with the numbers 1423. The message is ILNPAACENRIRCEAH. Your key word has 4 letters and your message has 16, so you will need to write out the message in a square of 4 rows of letters of 4 letters each. There are no nulls. Since B is number 1, write the first group of letters thus:

I			
L			
N			
P			

U is the second letter of the key and has the number four. Your next column of letters should be the fourth group. Follow that with G, the third letter, group 2, and S, the fourth letter, group 3, so that your square should work out like this:

I	C	A	N
L	E	A	R
N	A	C	I
P	H	E	R

Now you are ready to solve one on your own. Key word: BUGS. Message: CBEVTDOMOOEKOUWORNEN. Write it out in a square of five rows of four letters each. There are no nulls. The solution is at the bottom of the page.

There are many variations of these cipher squares. The title of Chapter 3 of this book is designed in a square of three rows of five letters each, based on the key word MUSIC. You can experiment with variations of the cipher square in the exercise section at the end of the book.

MESSAGES WITHIN MESSAGES

In the sixteenth century, an Italian doctor and mathematician named Girolamo Cardano invented a cipher system that is still used today. It is called the Cardano Grill. A grill is a pattern of squares. This is one type of cipher which puts a message within a message. A message within a message does not scramble letters exactly, but hides them so that when they are found, they spell out something quite different from the message that hides them. Here is how the Cardano Grill works.

Take a piece of graph paper or draw your own grill, and cut holes out of the paper here and there, in any pattern. Cut as many holes as there are letters in your message. Number the holes in jumbled order. Place the grill over a blank sheet of paper. Beginning with hole number 1, write the first letter of your message through the hole. Through hole number 2, write the second letter, and so on, until your message is complete. Then remove the grill and write a harmless paragraph around the letters of your secret message. The receiver of your message will have an exact copy of your grill and will place it over the paragraph to get the secret message.

Solution: CODE BROKEN MOVE OUT NOW

Let's say your message is ESCAPE AT ONCE. You will cut 12 holes out of a piece of graph paper in a pattern that might look like this:

```
        12            10          5
        ☐             ☐           ☐
        8        9    4
        ☐        ☐    ☐
    7
    ☐
        11   2              1
        ☐    ☐              ☐
    6        3
    ☐        ☐
```

Write the letters of your message through the holes. Remove the grill and the paper underneath will look like this:

```
        E            N          P

        T       O    A

    A

        C    S         E

    E        C
```

Now write a paragraph around the letters. You could write something like this:

```
W E ' R E    H A V I N G    A    P A R T Y
F O R    T O M    M O N D A Y
M A Y    1 2    A T    8 0 0 P M
A T    C A R L S    H O U S E
P L E A S E    C O M E.
```

The receiver of this message would place the exact copy of your grill over the message, write out the letters and unscramble them according to the numbers on the squares.

Decipher the message below with the grill below. The solution is at
the bottom of the next page.

A N O L D Y E L L O W D O G

H A S J U S T D I S A P P E A R E D

U N D E R T H E W O O D P I L E

B E H I N D T H E G R A Y

F A R M H O U S E O N

K N O L L .

The grill:

12	16		15			3		13	
▢	▢		▢			▢		▢	

6 □   18 □   8 □

17 □   21 □   14 □ 2 □   10 □ 9 □

1 □   11 □   4 □

5 □ 7 □   19 □

20 □

The notes written around a secret message like this could be mistaken
for open code. Since the Cardano Grill is still used in modern cryptography, it is possible we could decipher the death notice mentioned
in Chapter 1 with a grill — providing we had the right one.

Hidden messages do not always have to be deciphered with a grill. Letters can be placed in a pre-arranged pattern within a letter or a
paragraph in a book. The sender and the receiver must, of course,
decide on what the pattern is going to be.

Here are two examples of secret messages hidden in simple letters or notes. One man, who could decipher the secret message, was saved. The other, who could not, was executed.

In England in the seventeenth century, Oliver Cromwell dethroned King Charles II and set up a new government with himself as leader. England was divided between those who supported Cromwell and those who supported King Charles. Those who supported the king were called Royalists, and those who supported Cromwell were called Roundheads because of their haircuts.

Sir John Trevanian was a Royalist imprisoned by the Roundheads. He was put into a tightly guarded room in a remote part of a castle. Other Royalists had been put into that room just before they were to be hanged. Sir John did not expect to survive.

The Roundheads must have been confident that no one could be rescued from that closely guarded room, because they allowed Sir John to receive mail. One day he was delivered a letter signed R.T. No one has ever discovered who R.T. was, but in that letter he hid a message that saved Sir John's life. Here is the letter. You may find it awkward to read, first because it is written in the English of the time, which is quite different from ours. Second, because it had to be written around the secret message.

> Worthie Sir John: — Hope, that is ye beste comfort of ye afflicted, cannot much, I fear me, help you now. That I could say to you, is this only: if ever I may be able to requite that I do owe you, stand not upon asking me. 'Tis not much that I can do: but what I can do, bee ye verie sure I wille. I knowe that, if dethe comes, if ordinary men fear it, it frights not you, accounting it for a high honor, to have such a rewarde of your loyalty. Pray yet that you may be spared this soe bitter, cup. I fear not you will grudge any sufferings; only if bie submission you can turn them away, 'tis part of a wise man. Tell me, an if you can, to do for you anythinge that you wolde have done. The general goes back on Wednesday. Restinge your servant to command. — R.T.

Solution: NOW YOU SEE IT NOW YOU DON'T.

As soon as he had read the letter and deciphered the secret message, Sir John called the guards and said, "I know I am soon to die. Please allow me an hour or so in the chapel so that I can pray."

Confident that no rescue was possible, the guards escorted Sir John to the chapel and left him there in privacy while they stood outside closed doors. They never saw Sir John again.

In the note from R.T. the third letter after each punctuation mark spells out this message: PANEL AT EAST END OF CHAPEL SLIDES. Sir John had escaped through a secret passage.

Some 300 years later, during World War II, a British double agent by the fictitious name of Harry Ordway was discovered by a member of the OSS (now called the CIA). Harry was not the kind of double agent loyal to one side. He was known as a "freelance double spy" who had allegiance to no one and would work for any side, as long as the pay was good. He was a traitor to Great Britain and the Allies. The American OSS agent tricked Harry into giving himself away to the British in this way. He said, "Harry, you do such good work, you really should be paid. I will give you a letter of introduction to Sir William of Force 45" (the British Spy Agency). "I'm sure he'll be happy to see you."

The delighted Harry carried the letter to Sir William, presented it and sat back waiting for congratulations and a handsome award. Instead, Sir William read the note and immediately ordered Harry seized, taken outside, and shot on the spot. This is what the letter said:

SIR HARRY ORDWAY OFTEN TELLS THINGS HELPFUL IN SOLVING MOVEMENTS ARTILLERY. NECESSARY ARRANGE TERMS OF NEW COMPENSATION EMPLOYMENT.

If you read the first letter of each word in that note you will see why Sir William ordered Harry shot.

One weakness of open code and transposition ciphers is that very often the language looks awkward and is therefore suspicious. In the note about Harry the phrase "helpful in solving movements artillery" is not the usual English word order. It looks awkward. But in order to get the cipher to work, the OSS officer had to write it that way.

Another weakness is that a combination of letters or the order of words might be interpreted in more than one way. The result is that the deciphered message might say something quite different from what was intended. There was the case, for example, of the man going away on a business trip who asked his wife to get theater tickets for the night of his return. She did, and sent him a telegram telling him so. But there must have been a mistake at the telegraph office. When the man received the message he was both mystified and angry at his wife for spending so much money. The message she sent him was this: HAVE GOTTEN TICKETS. But the message he received was this: HAVE GOT TEN TICKETS.

In Russia in the nineteenth century, a man plotting to overthrow the government was saved from punishment because of the incorrect deciphering of a message. As punishment for his activities the man faced either instant death by firing squad or long, slow death doing slave labor in the icy wastes of Siberia. He escaped both.

The orders to punish him were sent by telegram. In a telegram the word STOP is often used to indicate the end of a sentence and is not to be considered part of the message. The telegram was supposed to read:
PARDON IMPOSSIBLE STOP TO BE SENT TO SIBERIA

But it was deciphered thus:
PARDON STOP IMPOSSIBLE TO BE SENT TO SIBERIA

DOTS, ZIGZAGS, AND MYSTERIOUS SYMBOLS

In a transposition cipher, A always equals A, B equals B, and so on. No matter where they appear in a message, or how they are scrambled, the letters of the alphabet are always the letters of the alphabet. Another kind of cipher is the substitution cipher. In this, you substitute other letters, symbols, or numbers for the normal letters of the alphabet.

Let's say you want to send the message CAT'S OUT OF THE BAG. If you reverse the alphabet where A equals Z, B equals Y, etc., your message will read: XZGH LFG LU GSV YZT.

If you assign to each letter the number of its order of appearance in the alphabet, A would equal 1, B would equal 2, C would equal 3, and the word CAT would be 3120.

If you use symbols, they can be well-known ones or ones you create yourself. A typewriter has keys with the symbols for number, cents, dollar sign, etc. If you use # for C, + for A, and ^ for T, CAT would look like this: #+^.

Another system of symbols is Morse Code, which really should be called Morse Cipher, because its symbols stand for separate letters rather than whole words. It is a system of signals tapped out by a telegraph key. The signals sound like "dit" for short signals and "dah" for long signals, which require longer pressure on the key. When the telegrapher hears the signals, he writes them down as dots for short signals and dashes for long signals. In Morse Code, C is — • — • (dash, dot, dash, dot). A is • — and T is — Therefore, CAT would look like this: — • — • • — — A complete Morse Code alphabet is in Appendix 3. Of course, it is not a secret cipher, because Morse Code is known the world over, and anyone can learn it. The trick is to take well-known symbols and use them in an original way. For example, you can make a double substitution. You could combine the reverse alphabet with Morse Code. In that case, you would write CAT as XZG and then put it into Morse Code. The message you would send would look like this: — • • — — — • • — — • Indeed, this type of double substitution was used extensively during World Wars I and II, when the air fairly crackled with codes and ciphers sent by telegraph in Morse Code.

Probably one of the most original uses of Morse Code was in the message that sank a battleship during World War II. The Germans were able to torpedo the British ship before she reached her destination because they received a message telling of her schedule. The message was hidden in a drawing of a castle along a grassy river bank. The blades of grass were made up of the dots and dashes of the Morse Code symbols for: QUEEN MARY DUE RIO MARCH 14TH 18 HUNDRED HOURS.

The advantage of using symbols for a substitution cipher is that once learned, they are easy to read, regardless of what language people speak or whether or not they can read or write. If you want to make your message really secret, it is best to make up your own system of symbols and share it with only a few people.

Criminals make up a group especially interested in secrecy. Back in the Middle Ages, wandering thieves communicated with each other by leaving messages of symbols written on walls, tree trunks, and fence posts. There were so many symbols the system was almost like a language in itself. Here are some examples:

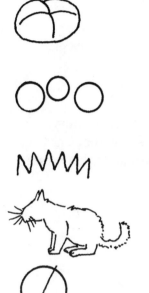

Hot cross bun.
Meaning: people here will give you food.

Coins.
Meaning: you might get money here.

Teeth.
Meaning: beware of dog.

Cat.
Meaning: woman living alone.

A broken head.
Meaning: easy place to rob.

There were others, which were not clear pictures, but had a definite, special meaning. Some of these were:

Avoid this place; people will make you work.

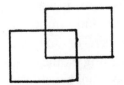

Threats and a show of force will get good results here.

These people fall for a hard luck story.

Only women living alone in this place.

Symbols like these were used clear into the twentieth century. Early in this century, a German criminologist named Professor Hans Gross prevented a robbery because he was able to decipher this message drawn on a church wall.

The first drawing is the crude drawing of a bird. It is drawn in one continuous line, meaning it is a signature. In this case, it was the signature of a criminal known as the Parrot. The second symbol is, obviously, a church. The third, the key, meant "to open" or "to break into." The symbol under the key is a baby in swaddling clothes, the Christ Child, and meant Christmas Day. The last symbol is a pile of stones and meant St. Stephen's Day, December 26. Stones were used for St. Stephen's Day because St. Stephen, the Bible tells us, was stoned to death.

Professor Gross understood this message to mean: The Parrot wants to rob this church on December 26th. Anyone interested in joining him meet here Christmas Day to make plans. After deciphering the message, Professor Gross warned the police to be especially watchful for suspicious characters loitering around the church on Christmas Day. They were, and the Parrot and his gang were caught.

A very well-known symbol of the Christian religion is the fish. Sometimes you see it expressed this way: ιχογε and sometimes like this: ⊂⊃ These symbols were originally secret ciphers. The early Christians were severely persecuted. They had to identify one another with secret symbols. ιχογε are the first letters of the Greek phrase *Iesous Christos theou uios soter*, which means, "Jesus Christ, Son of God, Savior." The first letters of the words in Greek also happen to spell out the word i-ch-th-u-s, which is the Greek word for "fish." Therefore, the symbol of the fish came to signify members of the then secret cult of Christianity.

It was not too long, however, before the cipher was uncovered, and Christians continued to be persecuted. Today, the fish is known all over the world, along with many other symbols of religions, nations, and organizations, including the Star of David, the American Eagle, the Red Cross, and many others. But as long as the fish was a *secret* symbol, it was a cipher.

Back around the middle of the first century B.C., Julius Caesar, Emperor of Rome, devised what is known as one of the earliest letter substitution ciphers. Caesar had a great need to write secret messages, because a lot of people were out to seize his throne and kill him. When he wanted to write a secret message he spelled out words simply by moving three letters down the alphabet. According to this system CAT would be spelled FDW. Of course, the word would not look exactly like that, because Caesar wrote in Latin.

Moving letters three spaces down the alphabet is almost as obvious as reversing the alphabet. Caesar's secret was soon revealed, and once it was, he abandoned the cipher. But it is still known today as the

Caesar Cipher, and certain versions of it are still used. The title of Chapter 5 of the book is written in a Caesar Cipher.

One of the people whom Caesar suspected of wanting to dethrone him was Cicero. Cicero had a slave named Tyro, who was a scribe. A scribe is a person who reads, writes, and keeps records for people who cannot do it for themselves. In ancient times few people could read and write; even kings, nobles, and the very wealthy were illiterate. So they hired, or more often enslaved, scribes. Cicero could read and write very well, but was unable to come up with an unbreakable cipher. He promised Tyro his freedom if he could create one for him. Tyro worked long and hard and finally designed a system of symbols that look very much like shorthand.

EMPEROR AUGUSTUS CAESAR

This system is still known today as Tyronian characters, but it too went out of use once it was revealed.

Cryptographers will tell you that there is no such thing as an unbreakable cipher. Once a secret is out, it is time to abandon the cipher and devise a new one. Any cipher — simple or complex — is effective only for a short time. Here are some other symbol ciphers, which today would be considered very obvious and low security, but which, in their time, worked very well.

The Rosicrucians are a philosophical society which began in the Middle Ages as a secret organization. They believed they knew all the secrets of the universe. They also believed their knowledge should be *kept* secret, so they communicated with one another in cipher. The Rosicrucian Cipher works like this: letters are written out in a grid:

A	B	C	D	E	F	G	H	I
J	K	L	M	N	O	P	Q	R
S	T	U	V	W	X	Y	Z	

Now, if you break up the grid you get a series of shapes like this:

A	B	C
J	K	L
S	T	U

D	E	F
M	N	O
V	W	X

G	H	I
P	Q	R
Y	Z	

to encipher a message, put dots inside the shapes. The shapes indicate the letter group, ABC for example, where the letter appears, and the dots indicate the letter itself. The position of the dots indicates whether the letter is the first, middle, or last letter of the group. In the message SEND HELP, S would be:

SEND would look like this:

The whole phrase would look like this:

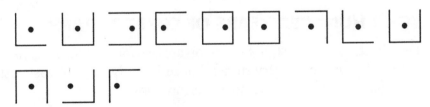

Decipher the message below. The solution is at the bottom of the next page.

The Rosicrucian Cipher was used for secret messages into the nineteenth century. During the American Civil War, Union soldiers in the Confederate prisons smuggled out letters enciphered this way. Another name for it is the Schoolboy Cipher, probably because of children's fondness for passing secret notes behind the teacher's back.

Someone, sometime in history, must have thought the dots looked like a lot of little pigs in pens, because the cipher is also commonly known as the Pigpen Cipher. The title of Chapter 2 of this book is written in Pigpen Cipher.

Secret messages can be written in a pattern of zigzags, lines, or triangles. To encipher this way, take a sheet of graph paper and write the alphabet across the top. Suppose your message is STAND FIRM. To write a zigzag, place a dot in the square under S. In the next row of squares down, place a dot under the letter T. For A, place a dot in the third row down under the letter A. When you have placed all the dots, connect them with lines. (See Figure 5.) To decipher the message, read from left to right, beginning with the highest dot.

To encipher the same message with parallel horizontal lines, draw a line from S to T. On the next row, a line from A to N. Next row, a line from D to F. Under that, a line from I to R, and finally, in the last row, a line from the far left to the letter M. (See Figure 6.) You could do the same with parallel vertical lines. Write the alphabet in a column on the left. Connect your letters from top to bottom.

To put messages into triangles, simply make a zigzag pattern and connect them as shown in Figure 7.

To make any of these messages even harder to decipher, you can blend the lines or triangles into a design or picture in much the same way the Morse Code symbols were blended into the picture of the castle by the grassy river bank.

FOUR HUNDRED YEARS OF CRYPTOGRAPHY

Dots, zigzags, and mysterious symbols are fine for fun and games, and are good to use in mystery stories, but serious cryptography is most often based on letter and number substitutions.

Two men are honored as the fathers of cryptography — Giovanni Batista Della Porta, an Italian, and Blaise de Vigenére, a Frenchman. In 1565, Della Porta devised a system of letter substitution in which one letter can be enciphered eleven different ways. In the modern version, which is shown in Figure 8, Della Porta's system is updated to the 26

Solution: HELP ON THE WAY.

Figure 5   **Zigzag**

A B C D E F G H I J K L M N O P Q R S T U V W X Y Z

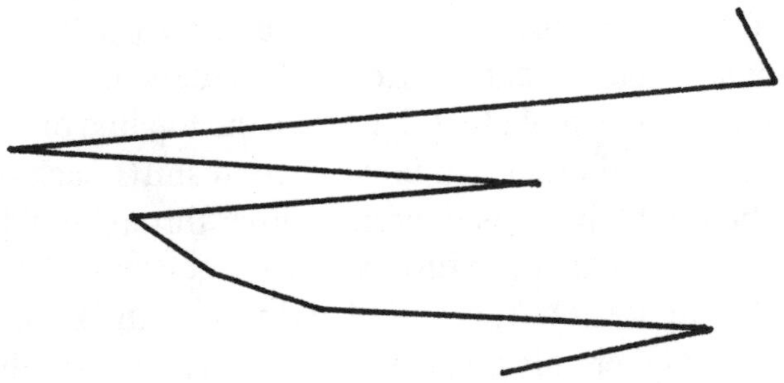

Figure 6   **Horizontal Lines**

A B C D E F G H I J K L M N O P Q R S T U V W X Y Z

Figure 7   **Triangles**

A B C D E F G H I J K L M N O P Q R S T U V W X Y Z

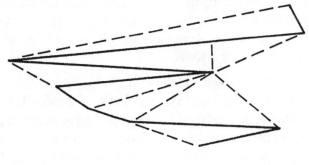

letter alphabet, meaning that one letter can be enciphered thirteen ways.

The letter pairs on the left are the key to the cipher alphabet to be used. Since there are 26 letters in the alphabet, there are 13 pairs, and therefore 13 cipher alphabets to choose from. The letters to the right of the key pairs are the cipher alphabets. Note that the top line of each cipher alphabet is in normal order, while the second shifts back one letter each time. The AB alphabet is in normal order throughout, but the second line of the CD alphabet begins with O and ends with N; the second line of the EF alphabet begins with P and ends with O, and so on. If you choose to encipher only one word using only one alphabet, and you use AB, the word PRISON would be CEVFBA. Each letter is replaced by the letter directly above or below it. C is directly above P, E above R, V below I, etc. But to write out a whole message you need a key word. Let's say your key word is NORTH and your message is SPIES IN PRISON. Begin by writing NORTH as many times as there are letters in the message, one letter over each letter in the message, like this:

```
N O R T H   N O   R T H N O R
S P I E S   I N   P R I S O N
```

The key letter over S means the cipher for S will be taken from the MN alphabet. The key letter O means the cipher for P will come from the OP alphabet. R comes from QR, T from ST, and H from GH. So the message will read: MIQNM OF HIYMHF.

The great advantage to this system is that the same letter is enciphered in so many different ways that it is nearly impossible to decipher it in a short time. Note that the letter I in the message appears as Q, O, and Y. Using a different key word, the whole cipher would be completely different while the table would remain the same. The great disadvantage is that one would always have to have the cipher table close at hand; it could be easily lost or discovered.

Blaise de Vigenére improved on the Della Porta Table by simplifying it so that it could be memorized more easily. In the Vigenére Table, shown in Figure 9, the letters to be used for the plain language message are written from top to bottom on the left, outside the square. The key alphabet is written across the top of the square. Inside the square, the letters of the top row follow the same sequence as the normal alphabet, but in each row down after that, they move one letter over, so that the second row goes from B to A, the third row from C to B, etc. The same is true of the vertical rows, or columns.

Figure 8   **Della Porta Table**

A B	A B C D E F G H I J K L M	
	N O P Q R S T U V W X Y Z	
C D	A B C D E F G H I J K L M	
	O P Q R S T U V W X Y Z N	
E F	A B C D E F G H I J K L M	
	P Q R S T U V W X Y Z N O	
G H	A B C D E F G H I J K L M	
	Q R S T U V W X Y Z N O P	
I J	A B C D E F G H I J K L M	
	R S T U V W X Y Z N O P Q	
K L	A B C D E F G H I J K L M	
	S T U V W X Y Z N O P Q R	
M N	A B C D E F G H I J K L M	
	T U V W X Y Z N O P Q R S	
O P	A B C D E F G H I J K L M	
	U V W X Y Z N O P Q R S T	
Q R	A B C D E F G H I J K L M	
	V W X Y Z N O P Q R S T U	
S T	A B C D E F G H I J K L M	
	W X Y Z N O P Q R S T U V	
U V	A B C D E F G H I J K L M	
	X Y Z N O P Q R S T U V W	
W X	A B C D E F G H I J K L M	
	Y Z N O P Q R S T U V W X	
Y Z	A B C D E F G H I J K L M	
	Z N O P Q R S T U V W X Y	

Figure 9 Vigenére Table

Code or Key Letters

	A	B	C	D	E	F	G	H	I	J	K	L	M	N	O	P	Q	R	S	T	U	V	W	X	Y	Z
A	a	b	c	d	e	f	g	h	i	j	k	l	m	n	o	p	q	r	s	t	u	v	w	x	y	z
B	b	c	d	e	f	g	h	i	j	k	l	m	n	o	p	q	r	s	t	u	v	w	x	y	z	a
C	c	d	e	f	g	h	i	j	k	l	m	n	o	p	q	r	s	t	u	v	w	x	y	z	a	b
D	d	e	f	g	h	i	j	k	l	m	n	o	p	q	r	s	t	u	v	w	x	y	z	a	b	c
E	e	f	g	h	i	j	k	l	m	n	o	p	q	r	s	t	u	v	w	x	y	z	a	b	c	d
F	f	g	h	i	j	k	l	m	n	o	p	q	r	s	t	u	v	w	x	y	z	a	b	c	d	e
G	g	h	i	j	k	l	m	n	o	p	q	r	s	t	u	v	w	x	y	z	a	b	c	d	e	f
H	h	i	j	k	l	m	n	o	p	q	r	s	t	u	v	w	x	y	z	a	b	c	d	e	f	g
I	i	j	k	l	m	n	o	p	q	r	s	t	u	v	w	x	y	z	a	b	c	d	e	f	g	h
J	j	k	l	m	n	o	p	q	r	s	t	u	v	w	x	y	z	a	b	c	d	e	f	g	h	i
K	k	l	m	n	o	p	q	r	s	t	u	v	w	x	y	z	a	b	c	d	e	f	g	h	i	j
L	l	m	n	o	p	q	r	s	t	u	v	w	x	y	z	a	b	c	d	e	f	g	h	i	j	k

Clear Letters

Clear Letters																									
M	m	n	o	p	q	r	s	t	u	v	w	x	y	z	a	b	c	d	e	f	g	h	i	j	k	l
N	n	o	p	q	r	s	t	u	v	w	x	y	z	a	b	c	d	e	f	g	h	i	j	k	l	m
O	o	p	q	r	s	t	u	v	w	x	y	z	a	b	c	d	e	f	g	h	i	j	k	l	m	n
P	p	q	r	s	t	u	v	w	x	y	z	a	b	c	d	e	f	g	h	i	j	k	l	m	n	o
Q	q	r	s	t	u	v	w	x	y	z	a	b	c	d	e	f	g	h	i	j	k	l	m	n	o	p
R	r	s	t	u	v	w	x	y	z	a	b	c	d	e	f	g	h	i	j	k	l	m	n	o	p	q
S	s	t	u	v	w	x	y	z	a	b	c	d	e	f	g	h	i	j	k	l	m	n	o	p	q	r
T	t	u	v	w	x	y	z	a	b	c	d	e	f	g	h	i	j	k	l	m	n	o	p	q	r	s
U	u	v	w	x	y	z	a	b	c	d	e	f	g	h	i	j	k	l	m	n	o	p	q	r	s	t
V	v	w	x	y	z	a	b	c	d	e	f	g	h	i	j	k	l	m	n	o	p	q	r	s	t	u
W	w	x	y	z	a	b	c	d	e	f	g	h	i	j	k	l	m	n	o	p	q	r	s	t	u	v
X	x	y	z	a	b	c	d	e	f	g	h	i	j	k	l	m	n	o	p	q	r	s	t	u	v	w
Y	y	z	a	b	c	d	e	f	g	h	i	j	k	l	m	n	o	p	q	r	s	t	u	v	w	x
Z	z	a	b	c	d	e	f	g	h	i	j	k	l	m	n	o	p	q	r	s	t	u	v	w	x	y

To encipher using the Vigenére Table, choose a key word. Find the first letter of the plain language message in the column at the left of the square. Follow that row until you find the letter under the first letter of your key letter. The point at which the plain language letter and the key letter intersect is the letter of your cryptogram. Using the key word NORTH again let's encipher SPIES RESCUED.

```
N  O  R  T  H      N  O  R  T  H  N  O
S  P  I  E  S      R  E  S  C  U  E  D
```

Find S in the column outside the square. Read across until you come to the letter N in the key alphabet across the top of the square. The point at which S and N intersect is the letter F. If you continue in this way to the end of your message, it will read: FDJX ESJVBRR.

To decipher a message written in this way, reverse the process. Begin with N in the key alphabet across the top of the square. Follow that column down until you reach F. Trace the cipher letters to the left until you reach the clear alphabet on the outside of the table. In this case the letter will be S, the first letter of the plain language message. Continue this procedure with the letters of your key word until you have the complete message.

Both these ciphers were considered unbreakable, and so they were, in their day. As a matter of fact, the Vigenére Cipher remained unbroken for 300 years. But they were time-consuming and awkward. During the nineteenth century, an era of fast advancing technology, when machines were being invented for everything, machines entered the world of cryptography. The need for speed and accuracy in sending messages increased as the whole pace of life increased. In 1832, Samuel Morse invented the telegraph. He devised his code of dots and dashes in 1838. Not only did it speed up normal communication, it was made to order for ciphered and coded messages. But there was still a need to decipher secret writing quickly.

In the 1880s the French produced St. Cyr Cipher, named for a military academy that had just been established. The principle is the same as the Della Porta and Vigenére Tables in the sense that it is based on a key letter or word and other letters are substituted for the plain language. But this simple device saved hours of time spent writing out complex alphabets. It can be made out of any stiff material —

cardboard, for instance — and small enough to fit into a pocket. This is how it looks:

And this is how it works:

The top alphabet is stationary on a frame. Inserted in the window is a strip of cardboard containing two alphabets. These are movable. To encipher, choose a key letter. Let's say it is Q, and your message is HIDE. Move the strip so that Q is under A of the stationary alphabet on the frame. Now look along the rest of the letters on the movable strip to H. H is directly under R of the stationary alphabet. So R is the first letter of your cryptogram. I is under S, D under N, and E under U. Therefore, HIDE is enciphered as RSNU.

Around the same time as the St. Cyr Cipher was designed, the Cipher Clock was invented. Like the St. Cyr, it can be constructed easily and made small enough to be hidden anywhere. It looked like this:

To make one, cut a circle about 3 inches in diameter and write the alphabet in reverse order, that is, counterclockwise around the edge. Cut a circle about 2 ³/₄ inches in diameter and write the alphabet in normal order clockwise around the edge. Fasten these two circles with a pin at the center so that the inner circle revolves. Cut a pointer long enough to go from the center to the edge of the outer circle. Cut a hole in the end of the pointer so that the letters on both circles show through. Fasten this to the pin.

Now here is how you use the clock to encipher a message. Your key word is MILK and your message is HIDE IN CHURCH.

Key:	M I L K	M I	L K M I L K
Message:	H I D E	I N	C H U R C H

The first letter of the key word is M. Find M on the outer circle. Chose any letter on the outer circle to tally with M. Let's use Y. Line Y up to M and place the pointer so that these two letters show through the hole. Now pick out every letter of the message which falls under M. These are H, I, and U. Find H, I, and U on the outer circle and write down the letters that appear beneath them on the inner circle. They will be D, C, and Q. As you proceed, your encipherment will look like this:

Key:	M I L K	M I	L K M I L K
Message:	H I D E	I N	C H U R C H
Cipher:	D	C	Q

Next, set the pointer so that the second letter of the key word is opposite the letter Y. Pick out the letters of the message that fall under I. They are I, N, and R. Match these with the letters on the inner circle. They are Y, T, and P. Place these next to the first cipher letters:

Key:	M I L K	M I	L K M I L K
Message:	H I D E	I N	C H U R C H
Cipher:	D Y	C T	Q P

Continue in this way with L and K. Your message will finally read: DYCE CT DOQPDB.

Throughout the nineteenth century and onward, more and more different kinds of cipher machines were invented. Shortly before World

War II, in the 1930s, the Japanese invented a machine that was very like a simple computer. The Americans called it the Purple Machine, after the Japanese Code Purple, which was mentioned in the chapter on wartime codes.

Basically, the machine consisted of two electronic typewriters. Since the Japanese alphabet consists of 50 letters and over 2000 Chinese characters, more than could be put onto any typewriter, the Japanese used the 26 letter Roman alphabet that we use. Each key of the first typewriter was connected to a system of plugs and revolving discs so that when the letter A was typed on the first typewriter, it could come out as X or F or Y or any number of other letters on the second typewriter. The same letter was almost never repeated. Although the Purple Machine was the most intricate cryptography machine yet devised, the Americans were able to reconstruct it and break Code Purple. Had the American cryptanalysts been able to notify the United States government of their discovery in time, the attack on Pearl Harbor in 1941 might not have been such a surprise. During the 1930s and throughout World War II the Americans, too, were constructing computer-type coding and ciphering machines.

Today, in the age of the computer, enciphering and deciphering are done in seconds. Infinite combinations of letters, numbers, and symbols are stored in computer memory banks. Other endless combinations of codes and ciphers must be known in order to access the stored information. The battle of hiding and discovering information goes on faster and faster with more and more complex machinery. There is today a cryptograph, an electronic typewriter, which automatically writes in cipher. Is it undetectable? No. Electronic receptors — bugs — can be sneaked into the typewriter. The bugs pick up the electronic signal of each letter of each key typed and transmit it to antennas hidden in the wall. The antennas carry the signal to a listening post outside. The listening post is equipped with more machinery which translates, interprets the signal, and recreates the original information.

But no matter how complex the hardware becomes, certain basic principles remain. Each new machine is no more than a variation of one that came before it. The computers of today are complex versions of the Purple Machine. The Purple Machine had elements of Thomas

Jefferson's spindle and wheels, and that simple machine was based on the scytale.

As to the ciphers themselves, it is true, as André Langie calculated, a group of 20 letters can be arranged a zillion ways, but it is no longer true that it will take 75 billion years to do it. Computers can do that job in no more time than it takes to type CAT on a keyboard. Nevertheless, the ciphers have to be created and understood. Someone has to program the computers. Someone has to have a firm knowledge of the principles of cryptography, and these too are basic. The Della Porta and Vigenére Tables were based on the Julius Caesar Cipher. The St. Cyr Cipher and Cipher Clock were quicker methods to put the Della Porta and Vigenére Ciphers into practice. The main difference between the scytale and the sophisticated computer is speed.

The most effective codes and ciphers are those simple enough for friends to solve *quickly* but complex enough to baffle the enemy *for as long as possible*. An effective code or cipher has to be secure. Security is only as strong as the intelligence and experience of the cryptographer who designs the cipher and the cryptanalyst who breaks it. Up to now, as far as we know, there is no cipher that cannot be broken eventually. On the next pages we will take a look at the principles of cryptography and see how some ciphers are broken.

3

KISACRBI PEGERNH
(Breaking Ciphers)

REASON IT

As we noted earlier, the most recent codes and ciphers are not common knowledge. Security is tight. The cryptography of World War II, for example, was not made public until 1974, and that war ended back in 1945. Most of what is going on today in the world of secret communication may not be available to the general public for decades to come. But we can guess that some of the basic solving techniques are still being used — not slowly and painstakingly with pencil and paper, but with lightning speed on a computer.

The most complex ciphers require code books, which contain definitions, patterns, and key words. Obviously, the easiest way to solve a cipher is to get hold of code books and key words. But usually code books are very well hidden and key words are changed frequently — in wartime sometimes as often as every hour. So cryptanalysts cannot assume they will ever get any clues or hints as we do for puzzles and cryptogram games.

By now you may have realized that it is easier to devise a cipher than to solve one. You, the encipherer, decide on the type of cipher to use, which key word to base it on, which way to express your message. The person to whom you send it or the person who intercepts it has to solve the cryptogram by working in reverse, piece by piece, letter by letter.

He or she has no idea how the message will come out, and for the time being, before it all falls into place, it looks like gibberish. Even with code books and key words to help, deciphering can be a long, dreary, sometimes maddening job.

With no clues at all, cryptanalysts must work by trial and error. They must use their intelligence, experience, and knowledge — if any — of the person sending the cipher. Today the job of the cryptanalyst might be made somewhat easier by computers that store information that can be drawn on. But the deciphering process still takes longer than the enciphering process.

Around the middle of the nineteenth century, a German officer, Major Kasiski, broke the Vigenére Cipher. This cipher had remained unsolved for 300 years previously. He was able to break it because he discovered something about language no one had ever noticed before. It was already known that languages use some letters more frequently than others. In English for example, E occurs most frequently, as it does in French, Spanish, and German. Next in frequency in English are the letters T, A, O, N, I, R, and S. REASON IT is an anagram for those letters. What Kasiski discovered is that languages also have patterns of letter combinations called digraphs (two-letter combinations) and trigraphs (three-letter combinations). TH, HE, AN, and RE are some of the most common digraphs in English, and CON, ENT, ERS, and EVE are the most frequently occurring trigraphs.

Kasiski reasoned that ciphered messages would follow the same pattern as the pattern of plain language, and that one could discover that pattern by counting the times certain letters, digraphs, and trigraphs appeared in a message. He pointed out that it was easier to decipher a long message than a short one, because in a long message there would be more opportunity to get an accurate count of repeated letters and letter combinations.

Other people took Kasiski's ideas further and discovered that one half of all English words begin with A, O, S, T, or W and end with D, E, S, or T. Furthermore, it was discovered that the most frequently used words in English are THE, OF, AND, TO, and IN. In diplomatic messages TODAY occurs with high frequency. Charts and tables showing the frequency of certain letters, digraphs, trigraphs, and most commonly used words were compiled. These charts are so useful to the cryptanalyst that western cryptanalysts have been known to solve ciphers even in Chinese without knowing one word of that language.

Frequency charts are in the Appendices of this book. Based on the discoveries of Kasiski and others who followed him, here are some ways to crack a cipher according to the principles of cryptography.

First, decide whether the cipher is a transposition or a substitution cipher. You do this by counting the number of times each letter occurs. If it is a transposition cipher, the most frequently occurring letters will be the letters in REASON IT, because these letters occur the most frequently in English, and a transposition cipher merely scrambles the normal order of letters, it does not substitute them with other letters. If it is a substitution cipher, the most frequently occurring letters will probably be the least commonly used letters in English, such as J, X, Q, F, or Y. Refer to the frequency charts to make sure you have guessed correctly.

It is more likely that the cipher is a substitution cipher, because substitutions are more secure than transpositions, usually. Although André Langie calculated that there are zillions of ways to scramble letters, letter and word frequency charts enable us to decipher an anagram faster than he thought, because they give us odds on what a word is most likely to be. For example, if you want to decipher HOGTRUH, a glance at the frequency chart will show you that T is often the first letter of a word, and Th is the most frequently occurring digraph. The odds are, then, that this word begins with TH. The chart also shows that words fairly often end in H, and OU is quite a common digraph. Having this information and using some trial and error method, it should not take you too long to discover that HOGTRUH is the commonly used word THROUGH.

Since it is more likely that a cryptographer will be working with a substitution cipher, here are some examples of how to solve one. Check to see if it is a Caesar Cipher. In that cipher, originally, words were formed by spelling them with letters three down from normal letters, or clear, as cryptographers call them. A Caesar Cipher today can be formed with letters any number of letters down from the clear. Suppose you receive the message: PJD NX ZSIJW RFY GD YMJ GFHP ITTW. To determine if it is written in a Caesar Cipher do this: Write the numbers 1 to 26 in a column on the left side of a sheet of

Figure 10

Caesar Cipher

	P J D	N X	Z S I J W	R F Y	G D	Y M J	G F H P	I T T W
1	P J D	N X	Z S I J W					
2	Q K E	O Y	A T J K X					
3	R L F	P Z	B U K L Y					
4	S M G	Q A	C V L M Z					
5	T N H	R B	D W M N A					
6	U O I	S C	E X N O B					
7	V P J	T D	F Y O P C					
8	W Q K	U E	G Z P Q D					
9	X R L	V F	H A Q R E					
10	Y S M	W G	I B R S F					
11	Z T N	X H	J C S T G					
12	A U O	Y I	K D T U H					
13	B V P	Z J	L E U V I					

				R			
				K			
				E			
				Y			
14					C W Q	A K	M F V W J
15					D X R	B L	N G W X K
16					E Y S	C M	O H X Y L
17					F Z T	D N	P I Y Z M
18					G A U	E O	Q J Z A N
19					H B V	F P	R K A B O
20					I C W	G Q	S L B C P
21					J D X	H R	T M C D Q
22					K E Y	I S	U N D E R
23					L F Z	J T	V O E F S
24					M G A	K U	W P F G T
25					N H B	L V	X Q G H U
26					O I C	M W	Y R H I V

graph paper. Write the ciphered message across the top next to number one. Now, under each letter of the cryptogram, write the letter that comes after it in the clear alphabet. When you come to Z, continue in the sequence beginning with A until you reach the number 26. If this is a Caesar Cipher you will begin to see clear rows on one of the rows. In the sample given in Figure 10, the message begins to appear on row 22. After deciphering two or three words you may stop at this point and fill in repeats of the letters you have already deciphered, as shown in the figure. Sometimes deciphering two or three words gives you enough clues to the rest of the message, and sometimes not. It is best to check your work by going down the alphabet for all the ciphered words

If you have filled in all the letters under all the cipher letters and you still do not have a sensible message, then, obviously, this is not a Caesar Cipher, and you must try something else. Now begins the long period of trial and error and process of elimination. The message is some other kind of substitution in which clear letters have been replaced by letters the cryptographer has just chosen at random, for all you know. Since you are not telepathic, you cannot read a person's mind, you must make guesses based on your frequency charts. Here is another message: SOOK WV MK KEJOO TH NEWJNE VUWMJO. Remember the high frequency letters REASON IT. Begin by making a tally of how frequently each letter appears, like this:

A B C D E F G H I J K L M N O P Q R S T U V W X Y Z
    /   / / /   / / /   / / / / /
    /   / / / / /   / /
    /   / /   /   /
                   /
                   /

O appears more frequently than any other letter in the cryptogram. E is the letter of highest frequency in English, so try E under every O, thus:

SOOK WV MK KEJOO TH NEWJNE VUWMJO
 EE   EE   E

K and J are next in frequency in the cipher, and T is the second most frequent letter in English. Try T for K:

```
SOOK WV MK KEJOO TH NEWJNE VUWMJO
 EET      T T  EE                 E
```

Now we have the three letters of a four letter word. How many four letter words end in EET? Run down the alphabet for first letters —BEET? Not likely, nor is FEET, the next possibility. The only possibility left is MEET. Unfortunately, there is no other S in the cipher to help us form another word. So now we look at the sentence structure. It is logical to try ME after MEET, but the letters don't match. IN, ON, or AT are logical guesses, but meet in, on, or at what? What two-letter word makes sense for the third word? We already have the letter T. Perhaps the word is AT. Write A for M. If you think for awhile you can see that the only logical word ending in EE to come after AT is THREE. Add the H and R in all places where it belongs. At this point, the message should look like this:

```
SOOK WV MK KEJOO TH NEWJNE VUWMJO
MEET      AT THREE    H R H S   ARE
```

Now let's go back to the second word. Meet what or whom? We have established it is not ME. Could it be US? Let's guess that it is, and write U and S where they belong in the message. Could the last part tell us where? If so, the TH might be IN or ON, so let's try N for H. So far we have gotten this far in the decipherment:

```
SOOK WV MK KEJOO TH NEWJNE VUWMJO
MEET US AT THREE   N   HUR H S  U ARE
```

Now look at the last word. It is easy to see that the only possible letter for the one blank space is Q, making the word SQUARE. As to the word before SQUARE, it begins and ends with the same two letters. H is commonly part of a digraph. Run down the digraphs in the frequency chart. TH is the most common, but that won't work. PH, SH, and GH do not fit here either. The only answer is CH, forming the word CHURCH. The word before CHURCH could be IN or ON. According to the cipher alphabet used for this message it is ON. The message is: MEET US AT THREE ON CHURCH SQUARE.

A word like CHURCH is a good example of why cryptographers have charts of digraphs and trigraphs as well as charts of letter and word frequencies. But these charts do not give all the answers. You have to be a good speller and have a good sense of the word order in sentences.

A great deal of the time you will be making guesses and trying them out to see if they work. And many times you will be wrong and will have to start all over again. It takes patience and concentration to be a good cryptanalyst.

Let's try another one. Let us assume that the sender of the message has not changed the cipher yet. You, the cryptanalyst, according to good cryptography practices, have kept a record of the cipher you have solved before. In this way, you have a head start, because you already know many of the cipher equivalents. You will have a sort of code book of your own. To keep a record of the cipher letters you already know, write out the clear alphabet. Match the cipher letters to the clear letters they stand for, like this:

A B C D E F G H I J K L M N O P Q R S T U V W X Y Z
M N O   E   S H T   U J V K W

Here is the new message: NEMHZO CPMHV UWXNRPG TJ OVNMCO XSCTVVXIPO. By assigning the letters you have compiled from the first cipher you should get a result like this:

NEMHZO CPMHV UWXNRPG TJ OVNMCO XSCTVVXIPO
CHAN E   AN S QU C   E SCA E M OSS   E

The rest of the message might just jump out at you at this point, and you might not need to do any more to solve the cipher. But if you cannot see the clear message immediately, follow the same procedure as with the other cipher. The solution is at the bottom of this page.

If these messages had been enciphered in numbers, as real life cryptograms often are, or in symbols, as mystery story cryptograms often are, the procedure would be the same. To make ciphers more difficult to solve, the letters or numbers are not placed in normal spelling order, but arranged in groups of four or five letters each. If there are some blank spaces left over in such an arrangement, they are filled in with nulls. Arranged in groups of four, the letters of the Caesar Cipher we solved would work out like this:

PJDN XZSI YGDY MJGF HPIT TWBQ

B and Q are nulls. To make it even more confusing, cryptographers will scatter nulls throughout the message. The title of Chapter 4 of this book is written in a cipher devised according to the Vigenére Table, key word MUSIC, arranged in groups of four letters each, in which the last letter or letters are nulls.

Here is another cryptogram based on another cipher alphabet. Let's try it with no other aids than frequency charts and what we can guess by the arrangement of letters and the order of words. The letters are not grouped in any special way; they retain the same length as the words in the clear, and there are no nulls. Since cryptographers are often helped by having some knowledge of where the message is coming from or who is sending it, here is a hint to get you started: It is a message you have intercepted from an enemy spy who has rescued an important person. The message:

GQNP GIRO IQP IX YIQHPMV TBPA ZOHOMSE PIFSV

Make a tally of the letters. You will find that the letters I and P occur the most frequently. Remember the most frequently occurring letters in English — REASON IT, or, in order of frequency, E T A O N I R S. If you try E for I, you will find it does not work in the fourth word, because there are no two-letter words in English beginning with E. T for I and E for P are possibilities. Let's try them.

```
GQNP GIRO IQP IX YIQHPMV TBPA ZOHOMSE PIFSV
 E T    TET  T E      E              ET
```

If this is correct, the Q might be H to fit between T and E in the third word, forming THE. But it is not likely that THE would come before a two-letter word. So start over. This time, try T for P. At the same time, notice that IQ occurs twice. It could be a digraph. A common digraph with T is OU. Could the third word be OUT? If so, the first letter of the fourth word would be O and we could have the phrase OUT OF. Try O for I. Now your message looks like this:

```
GQNP GIRO IQP IX YIQHPMV TBPA ZOHOMSE PIFSV
 U T  O E OUT OF  OU T         T  E E   TO
```

Solution: MUST MOVE OUT OF COUNTRY WITH GENERAL

Now it is time to consult the list of most commonly used words on the frequency chart. Look at the last word of the message. What commonly used five-letter word begins with TO? What happens when you fill in those letters in other places in the message? Continue looking for commonly used words that have the same letter patterns as the words you have partially filled in. With some more trial and error and continued referral to the frequency tables you can possibly solve the rest of this cryptogram quite quickly — perhaps in time to stop the enemy spy. The solution to this cipher is at the bottom of this page.

The cipher message was based on two key words. If you write out the clear letters A through F and assign to each the cipher letters of the message you will see that they spell out SLY FOX. Incredible as it may seem, really experienced cryptanalysts can sometimes pick up the key to a cipher before they have deciphered the whole message. If this happens, cryptanalysts have no need to struggle with the rest of the message through trial and error. Once they know the key words, they can determine what all the other ciphers will be. It works like this: Write out the key words. Underneath them, beginning with A under S, write out the clear alphabet.

Key: S L Y F O X

Clear: A B C D E F G H I J K L M N O P Q R S T U V W X Y Z

Now, continue from the X in FOX and finish the alphabet, leaving out all the letters that have already been used in the key words.

Key: S L Y F O X Z A B C D E G H I J K M N P Q R T U V W

Clear: A B C D E F G H I J K L M N O P Q R S T U V W X Y Z

Thus you have a cipher where Z=G, A=H, B=I, and so on.

If a message were enciphered according to this key, and the first two words of it were FADE BACK, the first two words of it in cipher would be XSFO LSYD. From that, some cryptanalysts might, just *might* deduce SLY FOX. They would realize they might be wrong, but it would be worth the trouble to try it, because solving a cipher with a key takes much less time than solving it through a long process of trial and error.

After years of experience cryptographers develop a sixth sense about language. Words and sentences seem to fall into place for them, as if by magic. Many so-called unbreakable ciphers have been solved on the basis of one or two lucky guesses. But if a cryptanalyst can develop a sixth sense, he or she can also go a little crazy. One World War II cryptographer remarked:

> Obviously staring at something which is completely mean-ingless and doing that for hours and days and sometimes weeks on end can be extremely boring... On the other hand you have to be alert all the time. It is a tremendous strain, a psychological and nervous strain. You get into the attitude where you see letters and figures everywhere and try to read meaning into them. Car numbers. Telephone numbers. If they begin with 66 and 44 then you think they must have some significance. It's with you all the time. You can't escape it. It almost sends you mad.

And indeed it does. Many cryptographers broke down completely from the strain of doing this kind of work under pressure of life and death wartime situations. After his work during World War II, one cryptanalyst spent six years in a mental hospital.

SHERLOCK HOLMES AND THE CIPHER OF THE DANCING MEN

Many mystery writers include codes and ciphers as important parts of the plots of their stories. In Arthur Conan Doyle's story, "Sherlock Holmes and the Adventure of the Dancing Men," detective Holmes breaks a symbol substitution cipher. The symbols are stick figures drawn in all the positions of a lively dance. By breaking the cipher, he uncovers the secret of a lady's past, solves a murder, and brings a well-known criminal to justice. The cipher was known only to the lady and to the prisoners in a particular jail. Holmes not only breaks it, he also uses it to encipher a message to the criminal, tricking him into coming out in the open. The story is a good example of how a cryptanalyst sets about the solution of a cipher.

This is what the cipher looked like:

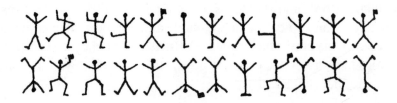

To decipher it, Holmes uses the basic cryptographic principle of counting frequencies. In the passage below, he explains to his faithful companion, Dr. Watson, what he has done:

Having once recognized, however, that the symbols stood for letters, and having applied the rules which guide us in all forms of secret writings, the solution was easy enough. The first message submitted to me was so short that it was impossible for me to do any more than say, with some confidence, that the symbol

stood for E. As you are aware, E is the most common letter in the English alphabet, and it predominates to so marked an extent that even in a short sentence one would expect to find it most often. Out of the fifteen symbols in the first message, four were the same, so it was reasonable to set this down as an E. It is true that in some cases the figure was bearing a flag, and in some cases not, but it was probable, from the way in which the flags were distributed, that they were used to break up the sentence into words. I accepted this as a hypothesis, and noted that E was represented by

But now came the real difficulty of the inquiry. The order of the English letters after E is by no means well marked, and any preponderance which may be shown in an average of a printed sheet may be reversed in a single short sentence.

Speaking roughly, T, A, O, I, N, S, H, R, D, and L are the numerical order in which letters occur...[but] it would be an endless task to try each combination until a meaning was arrived at. I therefore waited for fresh material.

Holmes, of course, does get fresh material, breaks the cipher, and solves the case by sending a message to the criminal in his (the criminal's) own cipher. It looked like this:

Explaining his work to Watson, Holmes says:

If you use the code which I have explained, you will find that it simply means "Come here at once." I was convinced that it was an invitation which he (the criminal) would not refuse, since he could never imagine that it would come from anyone but the lady.

When the criminal expresses astonishment that Holmes knows a cipher that only he, the lady, and his fellow prisoners could possibly know, Holmes replies, "What one man can make, another man can discover." And thus, the great detective sums up the race to make and break unbreakable ciphers, a race that has been going on for centuries.

THE ZIMMERMANN TELEGRAM

The decoding of the Zimmermann Telegram is considered one of the finest examples of efficient espionage and clever cryptography in recent history. Some historians believe it changed the course of World War I. Here is the story.

World War I lasted from 1914 to 1918. It was fought between the Allies, made up of Great Britain, France, and Russia, and the Central Powers, made up of Germany and other countries in central Europe. The United States remained neutral in the war until 1917. As a neutral country, the United States continued to trade with both sides in the conflict, transporting goods across the Atlantic Ocean by merchant ships. According to international law, neutral merchant ships in a war zone are not to be attacked.

As a neutral nation, the United States also allowed Germany to send messages via the telegraph offices in New York and Washington, D.C. This was very important to Germany, because early in the war the British had destroyed most of the other cable routes Germany could have used.

Great Britain's greatest strength in the war was her navy. Her second greatest strength, although few people realized it at the time, was the top secret work that was being done in an unimportant looking office known only as Room 40. Working in that room were a fashion designer, a university student, a literary critic, a German language expert, a publisher, and a lady who would later be known as "Aunt Elizabeth" on a BBC children's radio program. The one thing these people had in common was a keen intelligence and a talent for solving cryptograms. The only professional among them was their supervisor, Admiral William Reginald Hall. A brilliant spy and cryptographer, he was the one who had trapped the notorious German agent H-21, better known as Mata Hari. Under the leadership of Admiral Hall, the amateur puzzle buffs grew to be professional cryptanalysts of great skill.

Since the outbreak of the war, the British had been listening in on all German communication. As the war progressed, messages began to come into Room 40 faster than the staff could deal with them. This was long before the age of computers, and deciphering, remember, is a long and tedious business, especially without code books. But then, early in 1914, Room 40 got some help from an unexpected source. A Russian ship sank the German cruiser *Magdeburg*. As the Russian ship circled the sinking *Magdeburg*, members of her crew hauled up the body of a German seaman. Clutched in the dead man's hands was a German naval code book. Since the Russians were allies of the British, they gave the code books to the British Naval Office, and from then on, Room 40 was able to decode almost all the German plans for naval action. As a result, the British defeated the Germans in many important naval battles.

Nevertheless, British naval strength was quite evenly matched by the German fleet of submarines, the U-boats. These caused a great deal of damage to British warships and broke international law by torpedoing neutral merchant and passenger ships as well. The war dragged on. By

1916, both sides had suffered tremendous losses in manpower, weapons, and supplies, and the war had reached a stalemate. Yet the United States remained neutral. President Woodrow Wilson kept hoping for a peaceful solution to the conflict, and most Americans supported him, feeling that a war being fought far away had nothing to do with them. Great Britain very much wanted the United States to enter the war, and Germany very much feared that she would.

In January of 1917, Room 40 intercepted a telegram from the German government. Because the staff had been decoding German messages for over two years by then, they had some clues to what was in the message, but most of it had to be solved piece by piece, using all the methods of good cryptography we have already described. Once the message was decoded and passed on to the United States, it changed American minds about the war and perhaps changed the course of history. A diplomatic code, the message began:

0158 0075 4280 6321 9206 1783 5841 7390 8214 4569 4099 1439 3366 2479 4367 1783 4111 0652 5310 1139 8436 1284 9088 2895 2785 1139 8636 5731 7100 5224 8888 2785 2834 7009 1783 4852 4099

It was a number substitution code made up of 10,000 different groups of numbers which stood for 10,000 different words. But unlike the sample code shown at the beginning of this book, there was no clear rule or order to how the numbers were matched up with the words. 2479, for example, could mean several different things.

Although the Room 40 staff had some code books, they could not decode this message as easily as we might look up a word in an ordinary dictionary. The message was so scrambled that trying to decode it with the information they had was more like having a word's definition and trying to find the word. For example, if you had the word "read" but did not know what it meant, you would turn to R in the dictionary, find the word, and find its definition right next to it. But if all you had was "to take in by scanning" and were told to find a word for that definition in a dictionary that was not even in alphabetical order, would you know where to begin to look? That was one type of problem that the staff faced .

Another problem was the word order of the sentences. The telegram was, of course, in German, and German word order is different from

English word order. In English we say, "I went home." In German they say, "I to home went." Luckily, there was a German language expert on the staff, and once the German word order was understood and translated, the message seemed less scrambled. But the task of getting the full meaning of the telegram remained a long and difficult one. Only by intelligent use of the information they already had and diligent application of cryptographic principles were they able to put the whole message into plain English.

Look back at the code. Find 0075. This number might remind us of James Bond (007), but he had not been invented yet. 0075 was a sort of title of the message, indicating that it was a diplomatic communication. Room 40 had intercepted other 0075 telegrams, so that gave them clues to the meaning of some of the other number groups. They were able to determine that 0158 was the identification number of the telegram. 4820 told where it came from, 6321 and 9206 stood for the date it was sent, and 4852 was the name of the sender. 1783, 4099, and 2785 all meant STOP, that is, the end of a sentence. Once the code breakers found the stops at the ends of sentences, they were on their way to getting a sense of the whole message.

At this stage of the decoding, the message revealed this much: On January 26, 1917, Arthur Zimmermann, Foreign Minister of Germany, was communicating to 2479 that torpedo attacks would be increased, not only against British warships, but against neutral ships as well. Since this would probably anger the United States enough to enter the war against Germany, certain steps would have to be taken to keep the U.S. too occupied elsewhere to be of much threat to Germany.

Things looked dark indeed for the British. It was not certain that they could survive increased attacks by the U-boats, especially if they were cut off from American supplies. Admiral Hall wondered, what did Germany have in mind to cripple the U.S.? And to whom was this telegram addressed, he wondered, who was 2479? Hall realized that if he could uncover the identity of 2479 he would have an important clue as to what Germany was plotting.

Here is where luck and the cryptanalyst's sixth sense come into play. For some reason, history does not tell us why Admiral Hall *guessed* that 2479 stood for Mexico, of all places. Germany was communicating with Mexico about plans for action against Great Britain and the United States. Why Mexico? Mexico was neutral, had many internal problems, and could not afford to enter a World War. Here was a mystery indeed. And here luck played an important part. Hall was able to verify that his guess was correct and also discover the entire German plot in another German message which was sent in code 13042. Code 13042, as luck would have it, was much easier to crack than 0075. The plot was this:

Germany was inviting Mexico to join forces with her and declare war on the United States. In return for Mexico's alliance, Germany promised to help her recapture Texas, Arizona, and New Mexico, territory Mexico had lost to the United States back in 1846. Germany reasoned that if Mexico accepted the offer, the United States would be so busy fighting on her own southern border, she would not have the strength to aid Great Britain in Europe.

Without revealing the top secrecy of the work in Room 40, Admiral Hall was able to communicate the details of the German plot to the United States government. Since the Americans allowed the Germans to use American cables for their diplomatic communication, and Washington, D.C. had a direct line to Mexico City, copies of the Zimmermann Telegram were right under American noses in the nation's capital! But the United States did not know that. As a neutral nation the United States not only allowed Germans to use her cables, she also refrained from listening in on or reading German messages. By a series of complicated secret maneuvers, Admiral Hall was able to convince the United States government that Germany had taken advantage of American neutrality and goodwill.

Americans were shocked and then furious when they heard of the plot. Germany, they realized, was using American cables to plot against the American people and bring the war right up to their own boundaries. Within months, feeling in the U.S. changed from neutral to hostile. Woodrow Wilson declared war on Germany, joined forces with Great Britain, and by November of 1918, Germany was defeated.

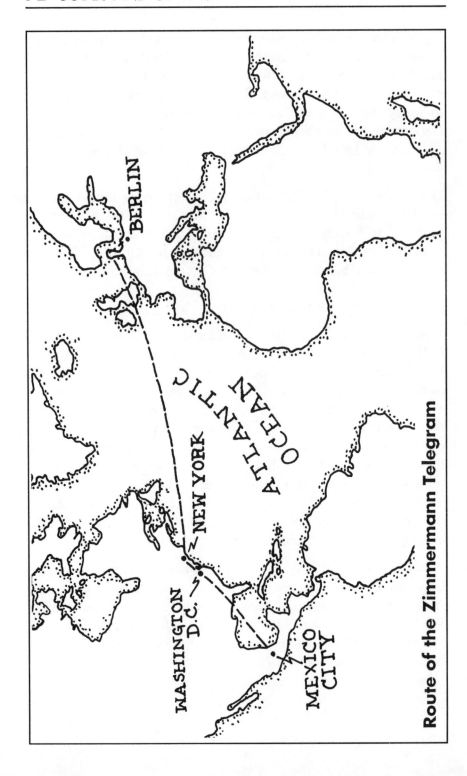

Route of the Zimmermann Telegram

4

EYFL KZAS VFTC VQPS MWKT QNEM UEUY MULB

(Sending and Hiding Secret Messages)

NOW YOU SEE IT, NOW YOU DON'T

Transmitting a message quickly and in secret is almost as great a challenge as devising an unbreakable code or cipher. Down through the ages secret messages have been sent many different ways. They have been sent through air on the legs of carrier pigeons, conveyed by waving flags or flashing lights, hand-carried by special messengers (couriers), sent through the mail, and broadcast by telegraph, telephone, and radio. They have been hidden in the most unimaginable places, sometimes "hidden in plain sight," that is, in places so obvious they were taken for granted and overlooked.

Lysander's slave, you remember, carried a secret message scratched on his belt. In some ancient societies it was the barbaric practice to shave a slave's head and tattoo a ciphered message into his scalp. Since in order to maintain secrecy it is the practice to destroy a message once it is read, you can imagine what happened to the poor slave if his hair did not grow back very fast.

In modern times we do not tattoo each other with secret messages, but messages are often hidden in clothing. A certain pattern of knitting or embroidery stitches worked into the other stitches of a garment can be a coded message. Messages can be sewn into secret pockets or linings or put into the hollow heel of a shoe.

During World War I, messages in code and cipher were sent mostly by mail and by telegraph. By World War II, some twenty years later, these methods of transmission were still much in use, but added to them were radio and telephone. Just as there has always been a race to see who could develop the most unbreakable codes, so there was a race to see who could send them fastest without detection. And a race to intercept messages before they could reach their destinations.

Censors and cryptanalysts have always intercepted and read mail to see if it contained any information that might aid the enemy. Anything containing numbers — business communication, for instance, or even knitting instructions, as well as telephone numbers, license plate numbers, dates, and the like — is studied very carefully. Crossword puzzles can contain a secret message, as can a drawing, a cartoon, a map, or a clipping from a newspaper. If a message is worded awkwardly, or contains odd words or much unnecessary punctuation it can be suspected as code or transposition cipher — a message within a message.

It is the job of the censor to cross out anything that might aid the enemy, even if the information is unintentional and the message is perfectly innocent. Censors have been known to cross out even the time honored XXXX OOOO, which means "love and kisses." Cryptanalysts, on the other hand, are on the lookout for intentionally secret messages. And once they find them they do not cross them out. Rather, they record their findings and send the letter on as if it has not been touched. This way, people exchanging the information do not suspect they are being watched, and continue to correspond until the cryptanalysts get enough information to uncover their activities and stop the operation.

Telegraph communication can be interpreted by anyone who has the equipment and knows Morse Code. By World War I, telegraphed messages in code were being intercepted faster than cryptanalysts could break them, as we saw in the case of the Zimmermann Telegram. Many telegraph installations had directional finders that could determine the precise location of the source of a message. Knowing where a message was coming from gave cryptographers important clues as to the kind of message being sent and the kind of person sending it — a spy in the field, a government official in a war office or an embassy, or a military person at a hidden post.

During World War II, radio and telephone came into their own as means of transmitting all kinds of information as well as secret messages. Open code was the method most used in radio communication, as we saw in the coded messages broadcast by the BBC during World War II. More codes and ciphers were devised. As fast as they were transmitted they were intercepted. As more information was intercepted, it had to be better and better hidden and the ciphers more cryptic. The race went on. Telephone communication was tapped. To get by the tap, telephone conversations were mechanically scrambled and voice transmission was altered. Of course, there were machines to do all of this — to encipher, decipher, scramble, transmit, and intercept. During the war Admiral Q (President Roosevelt) spoke almost daily with Colonel Warden (Prime Minister Churchill) by telephones which were equipped with voice scramblers. Yet the Germans were able to unscramble and decode a great deal of what they said to each other.

By the 1960s the technology of cryptography and communication reached an all-time high. There was a machine that could reduce a 350-word message to the size of a microdot not much larger than the period at the end of this sentence. This microdot was put on microfilm which was tiny enough to be hidden in a hollow tooth. Other machines projected the message back to readable size.

Today there are portable radio transmitters and receivers which can be hidden on a person's body or somewhere in his or her clothing. Voice transmission can be sped up so that it is no more than a few signals on the airwaves. Other machines slow it down again to the speed of normal speech. Satellite communication has made directional finders obsolete, that is, no longer effective. By satellite, communication moves so fast it is impossible to detect the source of a message. And for all of this secret information flying about, there are computers which encode, decode, store, and decode again.

The main disadvantage to all this electronic gadgetry is that it is so complex that if one tiny cog breaks down, the whole system can be wiped out. It is not wise to depend on it one hundred percent. There must always be alternative methods for sending and receiving messages.

A great deal of secret information still gets through the mail, because in wartime, the volume of mail is so great that it is impossible to get through it all, and in peacetime, there are laws against going through other people's mail. Nevertheless, anytime something is put down on paper, it is in danger of falling into the wrong hands. So cryptography continues to use all methods of transmission and cover — a combination of the oldest and newest methods. One method almost as ancient as ciphers themselves is the use of invisible ink. Invisible ink adequately meets the requirements of security, simplicity, and speed, which are necessary to good cryptography and espionage.

Any liquid that disappears when it is dry and can be made visible again by the application of heat or a chemical solution qualifies as invisible ink. Both organic and chemical substances are used. Organic refers to anything which is animal or vegetable. Organic substances that have been used are milk, saliva, sweat, and urine, as well as vegetable liquids, such as lemon juice, onion juice, vinegar, and wine. To make organic invisible ink reappear, hold the message up to the heat of a light bulb or candle flame, or the steam from a pot of boiling water, or press it with a warm iron.

Chemical invisible inks are made visible again by the application of heat or other chemicals, called reagents. Usually there is only one reagent for each chemical, but there are some reagents that work for several. Iodine is one of these. Simple H_2O, surprisingly enough, can act as a reagent for certain chemicals. During World War I, secret messages were written in a chemical that could be dissolved in water and were put into the fabric of clothing. When the clothing was soaked in water, the message was revealed. It somehow takes all the glamour out of the spy game to think that an agent could decode an important secret by the simple act of washing his socks.

During World War II, there was as much chemical experimentation as there was technological and mechanical invention. Chemicals were needed not only to write the invisible message, but also to make it visible again, and then make it invisible once again to keep the interception of it a secret. Since for many chemicals there is only one reagent, several reagents were put onto a special brush called a striper. This had several thick bristles placed wide apart. Each bristle was coated with a different reagent. If censors or cryptanalysts suspected there was secret writing in a letter, they drew the brush across the paper, hoping that one of the bristles would contain the correct reagent, and the message would appear. If it did, and they wanted to keep their discovery of the message secret, they would cover it up again with still another chemical.

Working with invisible ink is definitely a game of "now you see it, now you don't."

JOE K.'S HEADACHES

A fairly recent example of the use of invisible ink is the case of Joe K. Joe K. was an American who spied for the Russians during the 1950s. He posed as a leather merchant and sent much of his secret information in the disguise of business correspondence concerning leather sales. But he also sent messages in invisible ink.

When the FBI captured him, they found in his hotel room an enormous supply of toothpicks and a great quantity of Pyramidon. Pyramidon is the trade name of a chemical called aminopyrine, which is used in powder form as a medicine for fever and headaches. Joe K. claimed he suffered from chronic migraines, but the FBI knew that if he had taken as much of this medication as he claimed he needed, he would have already been dead from an overdose. They knew he had been dissolving the powder in water, writing messages with toothpicks and sending information to the Russians between the lines of his business correspondence.

"THE GOLD-BUG"

"The Gold-Bug" is a well-known mystery by Edgar Allan Poe. The story revolves around the discovery of a substitution cipher written in invisible ink. Without giving away the plot, here is a brief description of the gold-bug, a copy of the cipher, and the message it revealed. For what the message really means and what happens to the characters as a result of it, you will have to read the story.

The gold-bug of the title was a rare species of beetle. It was about the size, weight, and density of a bullet and the color of shiny yellow metal. On its back it had strange markings which looked somewhat like a skull, or death's-head, as a skull was called in those days. By accident, the markings on the beetle were pressed into a piece of parchment which was found near the place where the gold-bug was discovered. By accident again, the parchment came into contact with heat, and when it did, a mysterious set of symbols appeared on it. Le Grand, the main character of the story, and the one who deciphers the message, explains that the symbols have been marked on the parchment in an invisible ink made from cobalt oxide dissolved in nitric acid. Then, in good cryptanalyst fashion, he explains how he has deciphered the message. He suspects that it is a message from the notorious pirate, Captain Kidd, and might have something to do with buried treasure. Here is the cipher:

53‡‡†305))6*;4826)4‡.)4‡);806*;48†8¶60))85;]8*:‡*8†83(88)5*

†;46(;88*96*?;8)*‡(;485);5*†2:*‡(;4956*2(5*—4)8¶8*;4069285

);)6†8)4‡‡;1(‡9;48081;8:8‡1;48†85;4)485†528806*81(‡9;48;(88;

4(‡?34;48)4‡;161;:188;‡?;

Le Grand goes on to explain that he began by counting frequencies. Although the groups of symbols were not the same length as words in plain English, he was able to determine the meanings of enough of the symbols by some trial and error so that the message gradually fell into place for him. He established that 8 occurred the most frequently, and decided that it stood for E, the most frequently occurring letter in English. After that, he was able to construct a key containing ten more of the most important symbols in the message. The key was this:

5	a
†	d
8	e
3	g
4	h
6	i
*	n
‡	o
(	r
;	t
?	u

And here is the message:

> A good glass in the bishop's hostel in the devil's seat —
> forty-one degrees and thirteen minutes — northeast and by
> north — main branch seventh limb east side — shoot from
> the left eye of the death's-head a bee-line from the tree
> through the shot fifty feet out.

Although the message is now translated into the clear, it is still very mysterious. The rest of the story has to do with how LeGrand and his friends find out what the message really means, and how they act upon it.

This story was written over 150 years ago, and Captain Kidd lived nearly 150 years before that, so you can see how long people have been using invisible ink.

SUMMING UP

From Lysander and his scytale to Joe K. and his headache medicine, this has been a short history of secret writing through the centuries. There are quite a few books written on cryptography, but for security reasons, it is difficult to find much on recent developments. Cryptography is based on certain basic principles, however, which are probably still being used right at this moment.

The next section of this book contains some exercises in cipher you can do to test your skill with the principles we have described. Here is a quick summary of how to attack a cryptogram.

1. Have handy a bushel of pencils and a wagonload of paper.
2. Be prepared to make mistakes and start all over again. Get used to trial and error.
3. Refer to frequency charts. Remember REASON IT for the most frequently used letters in English.
4. Decide whether the cryptogram is a substitution or a transposition cipher.
5. If it is a substitution cipher, check to see if it is a Caesar Cipher.
6. Keep a record of the letters, numbers, or symbols you have deciphered in case other ciphers use the same ones.
7. See if you can detect key words or phrases the cipher might be based on.
8. Warm up by solving the Pigpen Cipher below.

5

HAHUFLFHV (Exercises)

Now you are ready to try your skill on some examples of the ciphers described in this book.

The exercises are designed for use with no other tools but pencil and paper. On your own you might want to make a scytale (page 28), a Cardano Grill (page 32), a St. Cyr Cipher or Cipher Clock (page 51) to encipher secret messages to your friends. Or you can always use the tried and true method of creating a message out of the letters in the printed text of a favorite book or magazine article. If you are good with a computer, you might want to use graphics software to devise messages in zigzags or triangles.

The exercises here are in four groups.

1. Pigpen Ciphers
2. Transposition ciphers
3. Substitution ciphers
4. A mix of both transposition and substitution ciphers

Once you finish, you will be thinking like a cryptanalyst and will have taken a first step into the world of secret writing.

PIGPEN CIPHERS

Make a copy of the grid on page 43 and solve:

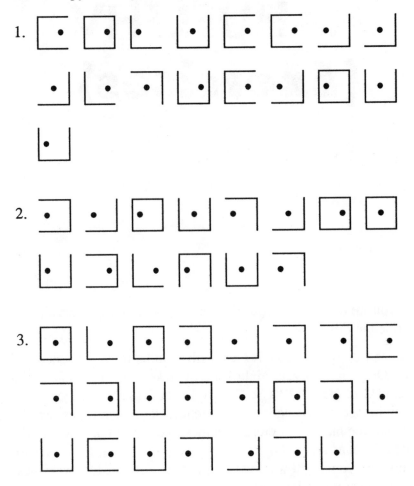

There is another form of the Pigpen Cipher in which the letters are indicated by numbers of dots, instead of one dot in the position of the square where the letter appears. If the letter is the first of the group, no dot is used. If it is the second, one dot is used, and if it is the third, two dots.

For example, RESCUE would look like this:

because, in their blocks in the grid, R is the third letter; E is the second; S is the first; C and U are the third.

CODES AND CIPHERS would look like this:

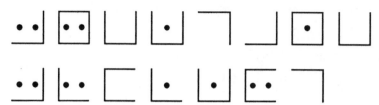

Try the following exercises. Solutions for all are on page 84.

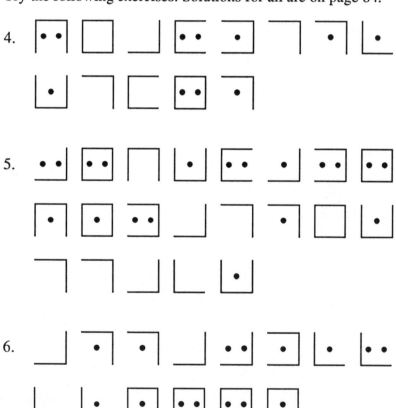

4.

5.

6.

Solutions to Pigpen Ciphers

1. ROGER RABBIT FRAMED.
2. JAMES BOND LIVES.
3. NINJA TURTLES TO THE RESCUE.
4. X MARKS THE SPOT.
5. COVER BLOWN. LAST MESSAGE.
6. ATTACK HIGH NOON

TRANSPOSITION CIPHERS

Transposition ciphers are deciphered by placing the letters in a prearranged pattern, usually a square or a rectangle. Often a null is used to make the message work out evenly. Sometimes the letter groups are arranged according to a number key. (See page 30).

The two exercises below are to be arranged in the squares or rectangles and are based on a number key. To make the ciphers easier to solve, the number keys used are based on the arrangement of letters in the first letter group in the rectangle, not on an extra key word, as shown on page 31. You will use two of these five keys: 53421, 21354, 14325, 24153, and 25341. Solutions are on the next page.

1. BLNCEX COOFHK DKTRNY ESIEGS OOSIAE

2. ATRTA BAPNV DHESN EREDE WEVAC

Solutions for Transposition Ciphers with Number Keys

1. Key: 25341 One null

CODE BOOK LOST IN FIRE. CHANGE KEYS X (null)

As a rectangle, the message looks like this:

```
C O D E B
O O K S L
O S T I N
F I R E C
H A N G E
K E Y S X
```

The number is based on the letters of the top line with B equal to 1, because it is closest to A in the alphabet, C equal to 2, and so on.

2. Key: 21354 No nulls

BAD WEATHER PREVENTS ADVANCE.

As a square, the message looks like this:

```
B A D W E
A T H E R
P R E V E
N T S A D
V A N C E
```

The number is based on the letters of the top line with A equal to 1, because it is first in the alphabet, B equal to 2, and so on.

The following three ciphers are formed in squares or rectangles and are based on patterns instead of number keys. The patterns are indicated by arrows showing the number of lines and columns and the direction in which you must read. Fill the letters into the pattern from left to right; then read in the directions indicated by the arrows. The number 1 shows which is the first letter of the clear message. Start from there and follow the arrow, reading from left to right or right to left or up and down. The ciphers are based on three of the four patterns shown. None of the ciphers has nulls. Solutions are on the next page.

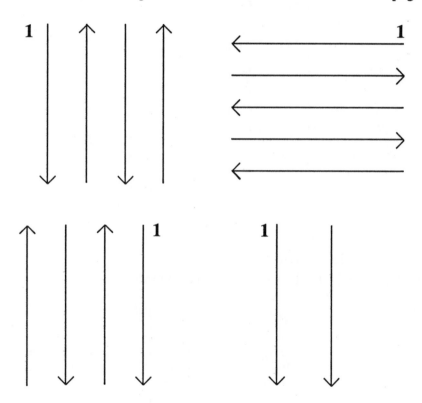

1. MDEI TSEG NUEI MSYE AWTO DRAK WEND

2. SEEG YHRA AOTN DUNG SSIM EESE UTTE

3. RTNEC ALHEA RAUQD TERSB DEGGU

Solutions to Transposition Patterns

1. Rectangle.   2 across, 18 down.
MET ENEMY AT DAWN DISGUISE WORKED.

Pattern: **1**

M	D
E	I
T	S
E	G
N	U
E	I
M	S
Y	E
A	W
T	O
D	R
A	K
W	E
N	D

2. Rectangle.   4 across, 7 down.
GANG MEETS IN TREE HOUSE TUESDAYS.

Pattern:

1

S	E	E	G
Y	H	R	A
A	O	T	N
D	U	N	G
S	S	I	M
E	E	S	E
U	T	T	E

3. Square.   5 across, 5 down.

CENTRAL HEADQUARTERS BUGGED.   **1**

Pattern:

R	T	N	E	C

←——————————————————————

A	L	H	E	A

——————————————————————→

R	A	U	Q	D

←——————————————————————

T	E	R	S	B

——————————————————————→

D	E	G	G	U

←——————————————————————

SUBSTITUTION CIPHERS

You will begin the following exercises with a code book of key words.
There are twelve key words and ten exercises. Some of the keys will
be used more than once. Some will not be used at all. Not all the
cryptograms will require a key. Here is your code book.

DINOSAUR

G.I. JOE

HOMERUN

JAMES BOND

RAPUNZEL

SPIDERMAN

THUNDER

TOM SAWYER

VICTORY

VIDEO

WALDO

WEAPON

Approach each cryptogram by taking these steps:

1. Check to see if it is a Caesar Cipher (pages 58 and 59, Figure 10).
2. Try out key words by writing out the alphabet as explained on
   page 60.
3. Check to see if the message has been enciphered using the Della
   Porta or Vigenére Tables (pages 47, 48, and 49, Figures 8 and 9).
4. Keep a record of key words which have already worked. They
   may be used again.

The first two cryptograms are written out in letter groups that correspond to the words in the clear message. The rest are written out in
groups of four, five, or six letters, some with a null, as they would be
in true-to-life secret messages. Solutions on page 92.

1. NHWR MHVVRE YX HMMYFXD YU BHQX DHTR
   MYGRB
2. GCTSG YSSH DH IDNW OBBF BA ZDHJFDX
   RTGHBFP YJGSJY

3. NSAFX NTSHM FSLJI YTSNS JFRBJ FYMJW UJWRN
   YYNSL

4. WSFG OYPZ CZAO YDZE OSYG JDZX XOCD SVWF
   SLAX

5. GRKAG OCTIL RIEAH MTDAS DGRHC BAGHX
   ATKAH ICZCG GCLQJ

6. LSDFSH FDCCSO JZOSFD FBNWBZ HRSTGX
   DZOHRD HHTYSA BFUBHV

7. WCPV DUSA RHPE ODHN ONNQ KNNH FPGZ

8. DBRH CFBR OFBQ REUY FBZH MRCX YBDP YUCR
   MYXE OHCR

9. ICPUB AJTUJ IJGKU XHPYV RSJAV ARIDA NADMB
   GNDGI

10. UBREW VPRGN SMNCM VNVPL RVDNU HWWUA
    NLMVU DLNPR CDSNJ

Solutions to Substitution Ciphers

1. Key: HOMERUN
GAME CALLED ON ACCOUNT OF RAIN. TAKE COVER.

2. Key: DINOSAUR
SPIES MEET AT BACK DOOR OF NATURAL HISTORY MUSEUM.

3. Caesar Cipher. Sixth letter down.
INVASION CHANGED TO NINE A.M. WEATHER PERMITTING.

4. Key: VIDEO
LISTEN FOR OPEN CODE IN TV COMMERCIAL SIX P.M.

5. Key: TOM SAWYER. 2 nulls.
RIVER BOAT WITH ESCAPED PRISONERS LEAVES TOMORROW *QJ* (nulls)

6. Key: DINOSAUR. 1 null.
WE ARE TRAPPED UNDER A ROCK ON THE ISLAND THAT TIME FORGOT *V* (null)

7. Key: WALDO. Vigenére Table. 2 nulls
ACE SPY SPOTTED AT ROCK CONCERT *GZ* (nulls)

8. Key: HOMERUN
TREASURE BURIED FOUR PACES NORTH OF SECOND BASE

9. Key: THUNDER
SPY CONTACT STRUCK BY LIGHTNING. SEND NEW ORDERS.

10. Key: RAPUNZEL
DRAGON CAVE LIES IN ENCHANTED WOOD BEHIND THE CASTLE *Y* (null)

TRANSPOSITION AND SUBSTITUTION CIPHERS

These last exercises can be either one or the other. You know enough now to be able to tell the difference. They are based on keys and patterns on the preceding exercise pages. Solutions are on the next page.

1. ACSEI EFHND IAGIL LRIDE NTTFS

2. OHDD VRZV HXCP QEER XQXP YVVY IOHC
   ROHV VOHD

3. CFXN BTRB MWAB WDLN BCLR GNPR XDFB
   NUXB MVPN CCRD NMEL DLSN GNSY

4. PALC AENS SNBO URRT IHEO DFTO WAEK LTVR
   EEPE

5. MVMU GTMI LMZQ LMVB QNQM LKWL MVIU
   MMUX MZWZ

Solutions to Transposition and Substitution Ciphers

1. Transposition Square.   Key: 14325
ALIEN CRAFT SIGHTED IN FIELDS.

1	4	3	2	5
A	L	I	E	N
C	R	A	F	T
S	I	G	H	T
E	D	I	N	F
I	E	L	D	S

2. Substitution. Key: HOMERUN
BATTLE PLANS HIDDEN IN HOLLOW BASEBALL BAT.

3. Substitution. Key: RAPUNZEL. 1 null
SUPER MARIO BROTHERS HAVE CAPTURED PRINCESS
AT EIGHTH LEVEL.

4. Transposition Rectangle. 2 across, 18 down.

PLANS BURIED TWELVE PACES NORTH OF OAK TREE.

Pattern: **1**

P	A
L	C
A	E
N	S
S	N
B	O
U	R
R	T
I	H
E	O
D	F
T	O
W	A
E	K
L	T
V	R
E	E
P	E

5. Caesar Cipher. 9th letter down.

ENEMY LEADER IDENTIFIED. CODE NAME EMPEROR.

APPENDICES

1. LETTER FREQUENCY TABLES

Most frequently used letters (in order)

E, T, A, O, N, I, R, S, H, D, L, F, C, M, U, G, Y, P, W, B, V, K, X, J, Q, Z.

Letters most often beginning words

T, O, A, W, B, C, D, S, F, M, R, H, I, Y, E, G, L, N, P, U, J, K.

Letters most often ending words

E, S, T, D, N, R, Y, F, L, O, G, H, A, K, M, P, U, W.

Most frequently used digraphs

th, er, on, an, re, he, in, ed, nd, ha, at, en, es, of, nt, ea, ti, to, it, io, le, is, ou, ar, as, de, rt, ve.

Most frequently used trigraphs

the, and, tha, ent, ion, tio, for, nde, has, nce, tis, oft, men.

Most frequently used doubles

ss, ee, tt, ff, ll, mm, oo.

2. WORD FREQUENCY TABLES

Two-letter words

of, to, in, it, is, be, as, at, so, we, he, by, or, on, do, if, me, my, up, an, go, no, us, am

Three-letter words

the, and, for, are, but, not, you, all, any, can, had, her, was, one, our, out, day, get, has, him, his, how, man, new, now, old, see, two, way, who, boy, did, its, let, put, say, she, too, use

Four-letter words

that, with, have, this, will, your, from, they, know, want, been, good, much, some, time, very, when, come, here, just, like, long, make, many, more, only, over, such, take, than, them, well, were

Most commonly used words in order of frequency

the	at	more	its	days	well
of	which	so	no	every	where
and	but	when	only	found	while
to	from	had	over	general	years
in	has	may	very	her	before
a	this	today	you	here	between
is	will	who	into	last	country
that	one	would	most	new	debts
be	have	time	than	now	good
it	not	we	they	people	him
by	were	about	day	public	interest
are	or	after	even	said	large
for	all	dollars	made	since	like
was	their	if	out	still	make
as	an	my	first	such	our
he	I	other	great	through	take
with	there	some	must	under	upon
on	been	them	these	up	what
his	many	being	can	war	

3. INTERNATIONAL MORSE CODE ALPHABET

A • —	N — •
B — • • •	O — — —
C — • — •	P • — — •
D — • •	Q — — • —
E •	R • — •
F • • — •	S • • •
G — — •	T —
H • • • •	U • • —
I • •	V • • • —
J • — — —	W • — —
K — • —	X — • • —
L • — • •	Y — • — —
M — —	Z — — • •

Notice that the most frequently used letters, E T A O N I R S, have the simplest signals.

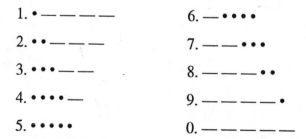

1. • — — — —	6. — • • • •
2. • • — — —	7. — — • • •
3. • • • — —	8. — — — • •
4. • • • • —	9. — — — — •
5. • • • • •	0. — — — — —

Notice that numbers one through five each have a corresponding number of dots with a decreasing number of dashes, and for numbers six through zero, the pattern is reversed.

4. SUGGESTIONS FOR FURTHER READING

George J. Church, "Crawling with Bugs," *Time* Magazine, April 20, 1987.

Arthur Conan Doyle, "The Adventure of the Dancing Men."

Marguerite Johnson, "Spies, Spies, and More Spies," *Time* Magazine, September 9, 1985.

John Laffin, *Codes and Ciphers.* Abelard-Schuman, 1964.

Dan Tyler More, *Cloak and Cipher.* Bobbs-Merrill, 1962.

Bruce Norman, *Secret Warfare.* Acropolis Books, 1973.

Edgar Allan Poe, "The Gold-Bug."

Walter Shapiro, "The Art of High Tech Snooping," *Time* Magazine, April 20, 1987.

James Raymond Wolfe, *Secret Writing.* McGraw Hill, 1970.

Index